THE TRUTH WILL SET YOU FREE

The Truth Will Set You Free
Exposing the Lies That Shape Your Identity

Tara Oldridge

©2026 All Rights Reserved. No portion of this book may be reproduced, stored in a retrieval system, or transmitted in any form or by any means—electronic, mechanical, photocopy, recording, scanning, or other—except for brief quotations in critical reviews or articles without the prior permission of the author.

Published by Game Changer Publishing

Paperback ISBN: 979-8-90158-072-1
Hardcover ISBN: 979-8-90158-073-8
Digital ISBN: 979-8-90158-074-5

www.GameChangerPublishing.com

To my parents, Douglas and Carol,

For the love you gave, the pain you carried, and the stories you lived before I ever took my first breath.

For the lessons that shaped me, the prayers you whispered, and the battles you fought silently so that I could stand here, free.

For doing the best you could with what you knew, and for giving me the honor of watching God redeem it all. This book is evidence that nothing is wasted in the hands of a loving Father.

Through your lives, I learned that grace restores, forgiveness heals, and love never fails.

May this story bring glory to God and honor to you both.

With all my love,
Your daughter, Tara

READ THIS FIRST

Just to say thanks for buying and reading my book,
I would like to give you a special bonus!

7 LIES YOU MAY NOT KNOW YOU BELIEVE

Scan the QR code here.

THE TRUTH WILL SET YOU FREE

Exposing the Lies That Shape Your Identity

TARA OLDRIDGE

FOREWORD

When I first met Tara Oldridge, it wasn't at a conference, an event, or through mutual friends. It was through a divine appointment.

I had just released a video called "My Apology to God" on YouTube, a raw confession of my surrender, my awakening, and the realization that no amount of success could fill the void He could. A few days later, I received a message from a woman I had never met before. It wasn't a fan message or a networking pitch. It was a message of authority. She spoke as a daughter of the King.

Tara didn't reach out to flatter me. She reached out to remind me who I was, a son with power and authority over darkness. She shared scripture, she spoke truth, and she celebrated what Heaven was already doing. She told me to cast every demonic foothold out of my life and my home, to walk in dominion as a son of God, and to take up the authority Christ gave us to trample the enemy underfoot.

That was the first time I saw the fire of Tara Oldridge. Not the kind of fire that burns people, but the kind that sets them free.

What struck me immediately was that she didn't speak *about* God; she spoke *from* Him. Her voice carried weight because it came from surrender.

She wasn't preaching theory; she was releasing power. And from that first conversation, I knew this woman had encountered the living God, not in a sermon, not in a seminar, but in the secret place.

As our friendship grew, I got to know her heart, her family, and her mission. I've experienced the generosity of the Oldridge family firsthand—the way they give without measure, love without conditions, and carry an atmosphere of freedom everywhere they go. There's a purity in their leadership that's rare in today's world, and it all flows from one place: total obedience to God.

That same spirit of obedience fills every page of this book. *The Truth Will Set You Free* is not a self-help manual or another inspirational read. It's a call to arms for the sons and daughters of God to take back territory that the enemy has stolen. Tara doesn't sugarcoat deliverance. She names it, confronts it, and redeems it *because she's lived it.*

When you read her story, you'll see the fingerprints of grace all over it. You'll see what happens when someone stops trying to fix themselves and lets Jesus deliver them completely. You'll see what real forgiveness, healing, and identity restoration look like. This is not about religion; it's about revelation. It's about remembering who you are and whose you are.

I come from a background marked by abuse, trauma, and deep brokenness. I spent years trying to outrun the pain by building success. But no amount of achievement could undo the damage of my past. It took Jesus to do that. It took the truth, the same truth that Tara preaches here, to finally set me free. That's why this message matters so much.

Tara and I share a conviction that freedom is not optional for believers. It's the inheritance of every child of God. And it doesn't come through "self-love" or "positive thinking." It comes through repentance, deliverance, and the power of the Holy Spirit.

This book will shake every place in you that has settled for less than full freedom. It will expose the lies that have chained you and point you to the One who holds the key. Tara writes like a watchman sounding the alarm, calling the Church back to holiness, truth, and authority.

If you let these words into your heart, you will not finish this book the same. You'll find your voice. You'll reclaim your authority. You'll remember that the same power that raised Jesus from the dead lives inside you.

Tara, thank you for saying yes. Thank you for standing unashamed in a world that loves compromise. Thank you for building The Academy at Lighthouse. Thank you for writing this book so that others might rise from bondage and walk into Kingdom freedom.

To the reader: don't skim these pages. Let them read you. Let the truth confront you, comfort you, and change you. And when it does, go change others.

Because the truth doesn't just set you free.
It makes you unstoppable.

—**Ray Higdon,** Author of *Faith Driven Wealth*

TABLE OF CONTENTS

Introduction – The Lies We Live Under 1

Chapter 1 – The Lies That Named Me 9

Chapter 2 – The House That Wasn't Home 23

Chapter 3 – The False Refuge 33

Chapter 4 – The Basement 47

Chapter 5 – The Illusion of a Fresh Start 53

Chapter 6 – The Attack 63

Chapter 7 – Pain Recognizes Itself 75

Chapter 8 – Good News & Demons of Light 85

Chapter 9 – The Night of the Reckoning 97

Chapter 10 – The Girl Who Went to Sea 105

Chapter 11 – The Mask of Freedom 113

Chapter 12 – Divine Mercy and Second Chances 121

Chapter 13 – The Truth That Set Me Free 131

Chapter 14 – The Birth of Lighthouse 141

Chapter 15 – The Upper Room 149

Chapter 16 – The Commandment of Freedom 155

Chapter 17 – Redeeming the Ground 167

Chapter 18 – When the Fire Fell 175

Chapter 19 – The Commission: The Fire Still Falls 183

Conclusion – I Still Hate Goodbyes 191

INTRODUCTION
THE LIES WE LIVE UNDER

I have seen the same lies surface again and again in the lives of my students, no matter their age, background, or how long they have called themselves Christians.

"I'm not worthy."
"I'm stupid."
"I'm confused."
"I'm tired."
"I'm busy."
"I'm depressed."
"I'm anxious."
"I'm scared."
"I can't forgive."
"I can't do it."
"I'm alone."
"I'm unlovable."

Over the years, I've watched these words wrap around people like chains. Some wear them quietly in shame. Others wear them proudly, like a badge. But behind every phrase is the same root: **a lie straight from the pit of hell.**

The heartbreaking part? Many of these people believe in Jesus. They've said yes to salvation, but they are not walking in the authority of His promises. They've entered into agreements with the kingdom of darkness, agreements they don't even realize they made.

Think about this: your mother leaves you at twelve years old. She packs a bag, slams the door, and never comes back. In that moment, the wound is deeper than words can describe. The child inside you can't comprehend it, so you make agreements to explain the pain: *I am not worthy. I am not lovable. I am not special. I am not safe. I cannot trust.*

What you didn't know at twelve years old is that these agreements open doors. They are sins (unforgiveness, bitterness, unbelief) that give the enemy legal ground. From that moment on, the kingdom of darkness rushes in to affirm your new belief system. Every heartbreak, every rejection, every setback whispers, *See? You really are unworthy. You really are unlovable.*

And so you spend your life collecting evidence that the lie is true.

How Lies Are Formed

Your belief system, the invisible framework that determines how you interpret life, love, purpose, and even God, begins taking shape long before you are aware of it. From the moment you enter the world until about the age of eight, your brain is in its most formative state. During this sacred window of time, every word, every look, every tone, every embrace or absence, every wound, and every wonder silently informs your soul who you are and what you're worth.

The human brain in those early years functions much like fertile soil. Whatever is planted, words of life or words of limitation, begins to take root. Scientists tell us that a child's brain operates primarily in **theta and alpha brainwave states** during this period, the same slow, receptive frequencies that adults experience in deep meditation or prayer. It is a state of open absorption, where experiences bypass logic and settle directly into the subconscious mind.

This is why Jesus said, *"Unless you become like little children, you will never enter the kingdom of heaven"* (Matthew 18:3). Children live from the heart; they are receptive and trusting. They don't analyze love; they simply receive it. But in that openness also lies vulnerability. Every expression of affection, every correction, and every silence writes invisible code within the child's developing mind. A gentle word becomes a belief: *I am loved.* A harsh word becomes a belief: *I am a disappointment.* A parent's absence can whisper a lifelong message: *Love leaves.*

Neuroscience confirms what Scripture has revealed all along: *"As a man thinks in his heart, so is he"* (Proverbs 23:7). The heart in biblical language is not merely emotion; it is the inner operating system, what we might now call the subconscious mind. Between birth and age eight, that inner system is being written.

As the brain develops, it undergoes a process known as **synaptic pruning**, strengthening the neural pathways that are used often and cutting away those that are not. Experiences of safety, affection, and encouragement become reinforced connections that teach the brain: *the world is safe, I am* *seen, and I am capable.* But when fear, shame, or inconsistency dominates, the brain wires for protection instead of trust. The limbic system (the emotional center of the brain) records these patterns like emotional fingerprints. This is why an adult can logically know they are loved and yet still feel unsafe in intimacy; the emotional memory was written before words ever formed.

God designed the mind with a remarkable system called mirror neurons, which allow us to reflect what we see. This is how children learn empathy, language, and behavior. They become mirrors of their environment. It's what Deuteronomy 6:6–7 foreshadowed when it said, *"These commandments that I give you today are to be on your hearts. Impress them on your children. Talk about them when you sit at home and when you walk along the road."* God understood that what children consistently see and hear becomes what they believe and become.

But what about when love was missing? What about when words weren't spoken, or when pain filled the silence? Science and Scripture agree that absence forms its own kind of presence. The lack of nurture or affirmation can imprint a message as deeply as an overt wound. The child learns to adapt. *If I'm not noticed, I must not matter. If love hurts, I'll protect myself by never needing it.* Those conclusions become the mind's survival code, useful once but confining later.

David wrote, *"Surely you desire truth in the innermost being"* (Psalm 51:6). Those "innermost places" are exactly where the false conclusions of childhood settle. Yet the same God who formed the mind also gave it the gift of renewal. The brain's capacity for neuroplasticity, its ability to rewire and form new connections, mirrors the spiritual truth of *"Be transformed by the renewing of your mind"* (Romans 12:2). Transformation is not wishful thinking; it is biological and spiritual reality. New experiences of love, truth, and safety can literally reshape the brain's pathways and rewrite the heart's story.

Healing, then, is both spiritual and scientific. Prayer, meditation on Scripture, healthy relationships, and honest reflection activate the same neurological systems that form new patterns of thought and emotion. *"Faith comes by hearing, and hearing by the word of Christ"* (Romans 10:17), and hearing truth repeatedly, especially in the context of love, has the power to replace fear-based wiring with faith-based reality.

What you believe about yourself and about God was once written by the voices around you. But those early impressions were never meant to be the final word. God, the original author, invites you to co-write the next chapter. Your mind is not fixed. Your story is not finished. The renewing of your mind is not merely a spiritual metaphor; it is a divine invitation to be rewired by truth and transformed by love.

Here's the danger: your belief system will defend itself at *all costs*. Once you make an agreement like, *I am stupid, I can't trust people,* or *I am unlovable,* your subconscious will collect evidence to keep that belief alive, no matter what. That's why people spend decades wondering:

- Why don't I have the bank account I want?
- Why can't I find the relationships I want?
- Why do I always feel tired, anxious, or depressed?

The enemy doesn't even have to work hard. He simply sits back, dangling your old agreement in front of your blind eyes while you squirm under its weight.

Neuroscience confirms that repeated fear and neglect during childhood wire the brain to anticipate danger, creating patterns that last long into adulthood. Emotional memories form before logical understanding, which is why adults can know they are loved yet still feel unsafe or unworthy.

But Here's the Truth

Jesus said in John 8:32 (NIV): *"Then you will know the truth, and the truth will set you free."*

The good news is this: you don't have to stay bound to those lies. You can break your agreement with the kingdom of darkness and step into the freedom, authority, and abundant life that Jesus already paid for.

This book is about exposing those lies: the lies humanity has believed since the garden, the lies I've seen plague my students in the training room, the lies that maybe you've believed your whole life. And then, it's about replacing those lies with truth. God's truth. The kind of truth that doesn't just heal a wound but changes everything: your identity, your family, your marriage, your finances, your future, and your eternity.

Because here is the choice God has set before us: "This *day I call the heavens and the earth as witnesses against you that I have set before you life and death, blessings and curses. Now choose life, so that you and your children may live"* (Deuteronomy 30:19 NIV).

It's time to choose life.

Neuroplasticity allows us to replace fear-based wiring with faith-based truth. Prayer, reflection, and repeated exposure to God's Word create new pathways in the brain, literally reshaping the mind and heart.

Can you recall moments in your childhood where, despite fear or neglect, hope appeared like a fragile thread? Perhaps a teacher, a friend, a song, or a quiet corner that made you feel safe? Those small moments are the first stirrings of transformation, a sign that even in brokenness, God's presence can guide us toward healing.

Reflection Question: Can you identify a moment in your early life when you first realized the world felt unsafe or that love was conditional? How did that moment shape your beliefs about yourself?

Journal Prompt: Write about a memory where you felt unseen, unheard, or unsafe. Then, write a prayer or affirmation to yourself, acknowledging God's presence and love in that memory.

Declaration:

I am loved. I am safe.

I am worthy of care, attention, and affection.

God's truth rewires my mind and heart every day.

Scripture Reflection: *"Then you will know the truth, and the truth will set you free"* (John 8:32).

Freedom does not come from trying harder or becoming better—it comes from **knowing** the truth. Jesus does not shame us for believing lies formed in pain; He gently exposes them so they no longer have power. Truth is not information—it is a Person, and His presence dismantles every false agreement we've made in the dark.

Scripture Promise: *"Do not be conformed to this world, but be transformed by the renewing of your mind"* (Romans 12:2).

Transformation is not only possible; it is promised. God designed your mind with the ability to be renewed, restored, and rewired by truth. What was once shaped by fear can now be reshaped by love. Your past does not disqualify you; it becomes the very place where God demonstrates His redemptive power.

CHAPTER 1

THE LIES THAT NAMED ME

I don't have memories of my parents before they divorced when I was four. What I remember is absence, the hollow spaces where love should have been, the echoes of arguments, slammed doors, and the quiet moments that whispered, *You are alone.* My father said my mother abandoned the marriage; my mother said my father had been abusive and unfaithful. I didn't have the words to understand, and I certainly didn't have the power to fix anything. The first lies nestled themselves in my heart: *I can't trust. I am unsafe. I am alone. No one loves me.*

Even at that young age, I could sense the tension, the unspoken danger, the instability that hummed through the walls. Can you remember the first time you felt unsafe, when the people meant to protect you failed, and your small body had to learn vigilance before it could learn trust? Scripture whispers hope in those early years: *"Though my father and mother forsake me, the Lord will receive me"* (Psalm 27:10). That promise, though distant and almost invisible to my child eyes, would later anchor my spirit in ways I couldn't yet imagine.

Weekends at my father's house were meant to feel like relief, a reprieve from the fractured world of custody arrangements and arguments, but at first they only amplified the fear. His trailer was old, grimy, and worn, with peeling wallpaper, creaking floorboards, and a musty smell that clung to the corners like stubborn shadows. The neighborhood smelled of burnt rubber, gasoline, and fear, a place where shadows seemed to move with their own agenda. I was terrified to enter the back room where his roommate, a heroin addict, lurked in a haze of needles and incoherence. I could feel a demonic presence there, though I didn't yet have the words to name it.

I slept in the same room as Dad, the rhythmic tick of an old clock the only sound that sang me to sleep. The fridge, more often than not, held nothing but the faint, lingering scent of forgotten leftovers, a silent reminder that I would have to find sustenance anywhere I could, even if it meant eating candy for breakfast while my father slept through the afternoon haze of his hangover. One morning, I did just that, too ashamed and fearful to tell him. Survival meant keeping quiet, keeping small, hiding fear, and navigating the chaos alone.

One night, I wandered out of my room into a living room filled with beer bottles and thick cigarette smoke, the air heavy with the sound of adults and their demons laughing and shrieking.

It was one of those weekends at my dad's house that always felt half-alive, the kind where the air smelled like stale beer and cigarettes and the sound of laughter acted as a thin, brittle cover for something darker, something I could feel but didn't yet know how to name, because my dad was living with his sister at the time and the two of them partied every weekend like it was their job, filling the house with blaring music, clinking bottles, and strangers who drifted in and out as if permanence were optional, the laughter loud but hollow, desperate, echoing off walls that seemed to hum with chaos rather than warmth.

I was looking for my daddy but couldn't find him anywhere. So I slipped behind the long drapes, hoping the fabric could shield me from the chaos around me. But even there, safety didn't find me. A shadow pulled back the curtain, and in that moment, something inside me shattered as someone lifted up my nightie to devour my little naked body like a starving wolf. I froze, screaming on the inside, but nothing came out. My sense of safety was replaced by fear and confusion. From that night on, I learned that I truly was never safe.

I was five years old the first time darkness came, wearing the face of someone familiar.

Even then, my body knew this wasn't normal.

I remember sitting still for long stretches, shrinking myself without realizing it, learning how to disappear into the couch cushions while my eyes stayed fixed on the television, absorbing images no child should ever see, my stomach tight, my chest buzzing with a quiet anxiety I didn't have words for, because I didn't know what was wrong—only that something was. The house felt unstable, like it might tip at any moment, and I learned early that silence was safer than questions, that watching without reacting was a kind of protection.

My dad was born to a logger in northern British Columbia and raised under the authority of his father, who believed he was the second coming of Jesus; he was not schizophrenic but rather a religious spirit so distorted that it bent everything it touched. He grew up in a household ruled by severity and fear, where living off the land meant growing herbs, refusing meat, and being forced to eat oats raw because cooking them was considered "worldly," where only wrath and judgment from the Old Testament were preached, and mercy was never named. And yet, in the quiet moments when his father wasn't listening, my Nana would read New Testament stories to him in hushed tones, and it was there, in secrecy and softness, that he first fell in love with Christ.

I didn't know any of that then, of course. I only knew the aftermath of it, the way love and confusion seemed tangled together in him, the way tenderness showed up inconsistently, buried beneath patterns he had never been taught how to break. Most weekends, he would have a new girlfriend, women who rarely lasted more than ninety days, sitting wrapped around him on the couch, kissing him openly while my dad's foster sister's son and I sat close by, pretending to watch movies but really watching them, trying to understand why affection felt so public and yet so empty.

I remember feeling embarrassed without knowing why, a hot flush creeping up my neck, a sense that I was witnessing something private without consent, something that made my insides twist with shame that didn't belong to me but somehow landed on me anyway. I learned to avert my eyes while still seeing everything, to dissociate just enough to stay calm, to build an inner wall where I could retreat and wait for time to pass.

The air in that house felt thick, heavy with confusion and a kind of moral disorientation that clung to everything, even the furniture, as though the couch itself had absorbed years of regret and was quietly giving it back. As

I sat there small and silent, absorbing far more than I should have been able to hold, something in me began forming, a quiet discernment, a knowing that what looks like freedom can sometimes be captivity in disguise, that noise can be loneliness shouting, and that love, when fractured, leaves children to make sense of adult brokenness long before they are ready.

That same darkness wore another face, too; I called him my cousin, but we weren't blood. His trauma ran deep. He was abused, neglected, and exposed to too much for even his young eyes. He had chosen me to be the one he experimented on. The one he would take advantage of.

He was eleven, old enough to know better, but just as broken as the rest of them. Looking back, I can see it so clearly now; the whole house was under siege. It wasn't just human pain; it was spiritual infestation. Demons don't need permission when alcohol and trauma have already opened every door.

That weekend was the first time something sacred inside me was stolen. And though I didn't have words for what happened, I knew it was wrong. I knew it was evil. I carried that silence like a stone in my chest, pressing it deeper every time I thought of speaking. Shame taught me that if I said anything, I would ruin everything.

That moment wasn't just an act of violation; it was an initiation. Not by God, but by the enemy. A counterfeit baptism meant to brand me with confusion and shame, to silence my voice, to make me forget I was chosen.

But the thing about the enemy is that he always overplays his hand. He thought that night would break me. What he didn't know was that God would use it to build an unshakable fire in me, one that would one day expose the same darkness that tried to destroy me.

It would take decades before I understood that shame is not a feeling, but a spirit.

And it was never mine to carry.

Yet even amidst this turbulence, small flickers of hope began to appear when, around age eight, my father hit rock bottom and began attending church. He wrestled with God, gave up the battle of his own way, quit drinking, and began serving others. The same trailer that had felt like a prison suddenly offered glimmers of sanctuary. Dad also began selling Amway products, and our weekends transformed into drives in beat-up $500 cars that any other child might have been embarrassed by, but I cherished them. Sitting beside him, listening to Dexter Yager tapes, Florence Littauer, and Christian music, I absorbed principles that would later anchor me in ways I couldn't yet understand. Being with him and learning from him became my first real glimpse that life could be different, that safety and love could exist in fragments, even in a broken world.

Life with my mother offered a different kind of challenge, one steeped in disconnection rather than chaos. Her house looked like a home, full of brand-new cars, a black-and-orange computer, and Pop-Tarts stacked in the pantry, yet it felt hollow, as though I were an invisible observer in a carefully curated set. The lingering smell of marijuana and cigarette smoke, with the soundtrack of her constant crying and the frustration and anger that seemed to coat every surface, created a world where I felt unwanted. I was often shooed from the room while she took business calls, her words echoing: "Go play. Go play. Go play." Those words made it feel as if sending me outside could replace the attention or connection I craved. Her first husband, much younger and emotionally disconnected, often bought love with orange soda and cinnamon toast. The house offered comfort in appearances, but the substance, the real, living love I longed for, was missing.

For all the chaos that marked my childhood, my mother's love had its own kind of quiet reprieve. It didn't always speak softly, but it showed up in Betty Crocker cakes, streamers, and balloons, in the way she made my birthdays feel like holy days.

She would make any cake I wanted. And not just any cake, but handcrafted masterpieces. She'd drive me to the local craft and hobby store, where we would rent shaped cake pans, and she would let me choose whichever one caught my heart that year. One year it was a rocking horse, another time a teddy bear, and once even Tigger from *Winnie the Pooh*. She'd spend hours hand-piping every swirl of icing until each character looked perfect, her focus unwavering. That was my mom, fierce, focused, and determined to craft joy even when she didn't have much to give.

On one birthday, we went to ten different gas stations just to find the perfect rainbow rocket sucker that looked like a unicorn horn because I was convinced the rocking horse cake *needed it*. She'd hang streamers from the ceiling, set out little party hats, and book the roller-skating rink so I could invite every friend I had.

I can still see her, standing in the kitchen late at night, hair falling from her clip, hands steady as she worked the frosting bag, humming to herself like she was building something sacred. She was. She was building memories that would outlast the pain.

When I think of her now, I don't see the anger, the tears, or the exhaustion that came later. I see the woman who bought a pack of Fruit of the Loom underwear for my sixth birthday so that all my friends could use fabric paint to decorate their own pairs, giggling as our little creations dried on the clothesline. I see a mother who tried, who gave what she could, when she could, and made magic out of ordinary things.

It took me a long time to realize that love doesn't always look like peace. Sometimes it looks like a tired mother, staying up too late, making cakes in the shape of joy, determined for her daughter to know what celebration feels like.

During that season, my one hope of comfort was my older sister—seven years ahead of me and a world apart. She carried herself with a confidence that felt untouchable, powerful in a way I didn't yet have words for. She spoke boldly about things she believed in, about injustices she noticed long before I understood them. When she entered a room, it shifted.

She had diaries filled with secrets I wasn't meant to read, boyfriends whose names I only knew from whispers, and bottles of designer perfume and hair products that lined her dresser like treasures. When she wasn't home, I would sneak into her room, pressing my wrist to the air, trying on her scent, her identity—imagining what it might feel like to be her one day.

To me, she was everything cool, everything grown, everything I wanted to become. I studied her from a distance, hoping proximity alone might make me more like her.

But while I admired her, she wanted nothing to do with me. And in that gap between who she was to me and who I was to her, I learned what it felt like to reach for belonging and come back empty-handed.

She would walk ahead of me, pretending not to hear when I called her name. I would say it over and over, desperate for her to turn around, to see me, to acknowledge that I existed. She never did. Only when my mother shouted from another room would she snap, "What do you want!?" as if even the sound of my voice was too much to bear. She would slam doors in my face, screaming, "Stay out of my room! Leave me alone! Get away from me!" pushing me forcefully, mocking me constantly, and even punching me to get me to shut up once and for all.

It may sound like ordinary sibling rivalry, but it wasn't. Not for a little girl who was starving for affection. Now, as a mother myself, I can see it clearly. This wasn't teasing or arguing; it was rejection founded in her own pain of sorrow and desperation. Later in my adulthood, she admitted she hated me for being born, that I ruined her life, and somehow, even then, I understood it. It may sound like ordinary sibling rivalry, but to me, it was the beginning of the lie, "I am not worthy." These moments can be devastating for a little girl who was starving for affection and clarity of where she belongs and who will keep her safe. Now, as a mother myself, I can see it clearly. This wasn't teasing or simple arguing; it was rejection rooted in pain far deeper than either of us knew how to name at the time.

Later in my adulthood, she admitted that she now hated me for being born, that my arrival ruined her life. And somehow, I understood. Not because the words didn't wound—they did—but because I could finally see the fear underneath them. The fear of being replaced. The confusion of not knowing where she belonged anymore. The quiet belief that she was no longer enough, no longer chosen, no longer safe.

What came toward me as rejection was born out of her own sorrow, her own unmet needs, her own sense of unworthiness. She wasn't a villain;

she was a child navigating loss without language, pain without comfort, and identity without reassurance. And in that place of fear and confusion, love can easily turn into resentment, and grief can harden into anger.

Understanding this doesn't erase the impact—but it does restore humanity. It allows compassion to exist alongside truth. It reminds me that broken people often wound not because they want to destroy, but because they are desperate to survive.

Forgiveness, then, did not come because the harm was small. Scripture never asks us to minimize pain or pretend that words and actions do not leave marks. God is near to the brokenhearted, not dismissive of their wounds. Forgiveness came because Christ is just—and because justice does not rest on my shoulders.

Jesus never minimized harm. He named sin plainly, confronted injustice directly, and still chose the way of mercy. On the cross, forgiveness flowed not because the offense was light, but because the cost was unimaginably heavy. Justice was fully satisfied in Him. That is why forgiveness does not excuse sin—it releases it into God's hands, where judgment rightly belongs.

Forgiveness did not mean reconciliation, nor did it require restored trust. Scripture is clear that forgiveness and relationship are not the same thing. Forgiveness is something I release before God; reconciliation requires repentance, fruit, and time. Even Jesus forgave freely and yet did not entrust Himself to those whose hearts were not healed.

So forgiving her did not rewrite the past. It redeemed my relationship to it. It meant I could hold compassion for her fear without denying the reality of what I endured. It meant her pain no longer had the authority to define my identity or dictate my future.

Forgiveness was not saying *it didn't hurt.*
It was saying *it will no longer own me.*

School was another crucible of fear. By the time I reached twelfth grade, I had moved eleven times, each one demanding a new version of myself, a new set of survival strategies. I was bullied relentlessly for being bright, outspoken, and pretty. By the eleventh move, the bullying had escalated to brutal physical attacks, leaving me with bruises and a reinforced belief that the world was unsafe and my value was conditional.

By the age of twelve, the lies of my early childhood had already settled in my soul: *I am unsafe. I'm scared. Love is conditional. I am unworthy. I am unlovable. I do not matter.* They shaped my understanding of the world, my family, and even of God.

And yet, even here, fragments of refuge appeared. Neighborhood friends offered laughter, companionship, and fleeting glimpses of being truly seen. Scripture reminds us that God's love is constant, even when human love falters: *"This is love: not that we loved God, but that He loved us and sent His Son as an atoning sacrifice for our sins. Dear friends, if God so loved us, we also ought to love one another"* (1 John 4:10-12). Even when the adults in my life failed me, God's love was waiting to meet me.

Amidst chaos, seeds of hope began to take root. My father's journey with church and personal development created moments of safety and teaching that contrasted sharply with the fear and neglect I experienced elsewhere. Those drives in beat-up cars, listening to tapes about faith, leadership, and personal growth, became lifelines. They whispered a promise: life could be different. God was faithful. I was not alone. These were early lessons in resilience, trust, and faith, even when my young heart could only grasp fragments of their meaning.

Through the church my dad had started attending, I went to a Bible camp that would become the greatest miracle of my early years. On the first night, the campers gathered in a small, moonlit chapel at the front of the room. The air smelled faintly of polished wood and hymnals, carrying the quiet hum of anticipation. I don't think I fully understood what was happening, but something deep inside me stirred.

As they made the altar call to receive Jesus as my personal Lord and Savior, I walked forward, my little heart pounding. I didn't know exactly what to say or do, but the moment I stepped into that sacred space, a gentle yet overwhelming warmth enveloped me. I wept, not from sorrow but from a profound sense of being seen, held, and loved in a way I had never experienced. Every fear, every lonely hour, and every rejection seemed to melt in that presence. The Spirit of God engulfed me, whispering truths my young mind could barely articulate: *You are chosen. You are loved. You matter.*

It was so beautiful, so peaceful, that I couldn't stop. The next night, I went forward again, not because I needed to prove anything, but because I wanted to stay in that embrace. I wanted to feel that same comfort, that same love, that was stronger than all the lies I had been told. I could finally sense, in a way I had never known, that Jesus was real and that His plan for me was beginning to unfold, even if I couldn't yet see it fully.

From that moment on, a seed of hope was planted deep in my heart. I had met the One who would walk with me through all the chaos and fear of my childhood, who would hold me through every rejection, every night of loneliness, and every lie I had believed about myself. He chose me. He found me. And in that chapel, surrounded by the soft light and the hushed prayers of others, a new seed was planted that, from then on, I would never be alone.

Reflection Question: Can you identify a moment in your early life when you first realized the world felt unsafe or that love was conditional? How did that moment shape your beliefs about yourself?

Journal Prompt: Write about a memory where you felt unseen, unheard, or unsafe. Then, write a prayer or affirmation to yourself, acknowledging God's presence and love in that memory.

Declaration:

I am seen and known by the God of the Universe.

He sees me. He hears me. He loves me.

I am fearfully and wonderfully made. Created in his image.

Scripture Reflection: *"For I am the Lord your God who takes hold of your right hand and says to you, 'Do not fear; I will help you'"* (Isaiah 41:13).

Fear often enters quietly, shaping beliefs before we realize it has a voice. What felt unsafe or conditional may have taught us to guard our hearts, but God was present even then, steady, near, and faithful. His help does not arrive with condemnation, but with compassion. The truths formed in fear are not permanent. In God's presence, they can be gently replaced with love, safety, and truth.

Scripture Promise: *"For I am the Lord your God who takes hold of your right hand and says to you, 'Do not fear; I will help you'"* (Isaiah 41:13).

CHAPTER 2

THE HOUSE THAT WASN'T HOME

When I stepped into junior high, fear became the hum beneath my skin, like a frequency I couldn't turn off.

I can still smell my stepbrother's basement. The air was thick with incense, marijuana residue, and the burnt-metal scent of guitar strings. The walls were plastered with rebellion, Motley Crüe, Metallica, and Nine Inch Nails posters curling at the corners. Red and purple light bled from a lava lamp, casting everything in a demonic glow. He would sit there for hours, hunched over his guitar, hair hanging in his face, strumming the same dark chords over and over like a curse.

Trevor wasn't just angry; he was *possessed*. I didn't have the language for it then, but I could feel it. The atmosphere changed when he entered a room. Even the air went still, waiting. His scowl was heavy, his silence louder than a shout. His presence pressed on my chest until it hurt to breathe. He reminded me of the Undertaker from WWE—pale, soulless, death in human form.

His mother had divorced his father for being physically abusive. But that spirit didn't die when the papers were signed; it just found a new host. Now, the spirit was living inside her son. The same hands that should have been tender became weapons. The same voice that should have comforted became cruel.

He didn't just pull my hair; he dragged me by it across the living room floor. He didn't just throw remotes; he aimed them at my face, the plastic exploding against my cheek, leaving welts that pulsed like heartbeats under my skin. He didn't just yell; he laughed, laughed like he enjoyed it, like my pain was music.

He smashed my Mariah Carey CDs one by one, cracking them in half while quoting lyrics back at me in mockery. He said I listened to "trash," that my music was weak, and that *I* was weak. Then he'd go back to the basement and crank his guitar until the floorboards shook. It was as if the sound itself was trying to drive out anything pure, anything light, anything that could still believe in love.

My dad would sometimes snap, yelling at him for his disrespect, for the way he treated us, but it never mattered. Trevor would just smirk, a slow, twisted grin, and walk away. He'd already given himself over to something darker.

The house was a pressure cooker of rage and exhaustion. You could feel it in your bones, like thunder trapped beneath the floorboards. Every day was survival. I learned to listen for footsteps, to gauge the tone of his breathing, and to disappear before he noticed me. I learned how to become small.

My heart would race whenever he passed me in the hallway. I could feel my blood rushing in my ears. My little body was constantly braced for impact, always waiting for the next blow, the next explosion. That kind of fear becomes a language you speak fluently when you grow up in chaos.

And somewhere in those long, trembling nights, I made a promise to myself. I said it in silence, but I meant it with every ounce of my being: *I will never need anyone. Ever again.*

That vow became my armor. I mistook it for strength. I called it independence. But it was forged in fear. It was my way of saying, "No one will ever hurt me again," not realizing that in keeping everyone out, I was also keeping love out.

I didn't know it then, but the enemy was there too, whispering agreement into my vow. That's what trauma does. It doesn't just wound you; it partners with lies. Lies that sound like truth. Lies that say, *You're safer alone.* Lies that say, *You can only trust yourself.*

For years, I carried that vow like a badge of honor. I built my walls high and my standards higher. I learned how to fight, how to charm, how to win, and how to never need anyone. I thought that was power.

But it wasn't power.

It was prison.

When Jesus came for me years later, He didn't start with my success or my calling; He went after that vow. He went straight to the little girl who made it, the one hiding under the blankets with a pounding heart and a split lip, praying to a God she had only been told was real.

And when He found her, He didn't say, "Be strong." He said, "You don't have to be."

He showed me that what I thought was survival was actually isolation. That the strength I thought I had built was just fear in disguise. That control isn't safety; surrender is.

It took years to undo what one vow had built, but when it broke, when that fortress finally came down, I could finally see it clearly. The darkness that once ruled that basement, that home, that boy, it wasn't just haunting us. It was hunting identity.

But it lost. Because even there, in that house of fear, God never left. Even when I couldn't see Him, He was standing between the enemy and me, whispering, *"Not forever, my daughter. I'm coming for you."*

Most mornings, I walked to school alone, tracing the same cracked sidewalk, breath hanging in the frozen air, backpack slung over shoulders that already carried too much. Sometimes I'd trail behind a group of girls who didn't really like me, pretending I belonged just long enough to look like I did. In our small town, *"Watch your back!"* wasn't just a saying; it was survival code.

And yet, even in the middle of all that fear, there were Alana and Cher. We found each other early, three girls trying to make sense of a world that often made no sense at all. From the very beginning, they were my safe place, the only thing that kept me from falling apart. We were inseparable: a trio stitched together by laughter, secrets, and teenage dreams too big for our small town.

After school, we'd crowd into Alana's bedroom, surrounded by magazine clippings of boy bands and perfume samples torn from *YM*. We staged photo shoots, sang into hairbrush microphones, prank-called boys, and laughed until our stomachs hurt. There was no fear in those moments, only the dizzy, holy relief of being thirteen and seen. For a while, that friendship was my sanctuary, proof that joy could exist alongside pain.

Still, the fear outside those walls never loosened its grip. For years, I had lived braced for impact, flinching at the idea of being hurt, humiliated, or targeted. By the time I entered eighth grade, that fear was no longer imaginary. It had weight. It had consequences. What once lived only in my stomach and my thoughts was beginning to show up in my body.

Someone told me a girl named Nicole wanted to beat me up. I didn't even know her. There was no history, no conflict, no reason I could point to. But reason didn't matter. The threat alone was enough to make me physically ill. My chest tightened. My hands shook. I scanned hallways and corners, waiting for something I couldn't escape. The fear had crossed a line. It wasn't just emotional anymore. It was becoming physical, real, unavoidable.

If it hadn't been for Candice, a quiet, kind girl who knew both of us, I don't know how I would have survived that first week of eighth grade. She became a buffer between rumor and reality, between what might happen and what hadn't yet.

By high school, this had become my new normal. Glares in the hallways. Empty threats whispered just loudly enough to be heard. Eyes that lingered too long, devouring rather than seeing me—boys my age, and older ones too. I learned to read rooms quickly, to stay alert, and to keep my guard up at all times. Fear was no longer a passing emotion. It was the atmosphere I lived in.

I lived on adrenaline. My heart pounded before the first bell even rang. Whispers followed me like wind. *Slut. Whore. Trash.* I didn't even know what those words meant, only that they made my stomach twist.

I tried to disappear, but I also yearned to matter. It's strange how survival can masquerade as confidence.

At home, the noise was different but just as sharp. My dad and stepmom fought constantly about money. The walls vibrated with frustration, the same arguments looping like a scratched record. My mother, meanwhile, lived two blocks away, close enough for me to see her house on walks to school, yet so far that her silence became its own kind of violence. She never called. Never checked in. Never asked if I was eating or sleeping or breathing. I existed, and she simply chose not to.

Once, when I was twelve, I asked her to sign a form so I could get my belly button pierced. She did, without hesitation or question. I remember watching the piercing gun flash and thinking, *So this is what her "yes" sounds like.* A signature for something meaningless, when what I needed was to know I mattered.

My dad adored me. He often said that the day I was born, he knew our bond would save his life. But his love for me only deepened my stepmom's resentment. She competed with me for his attention as if love were a pie to be divided. One winter day, when the air bit through our coats, my dad insisted on taking me shopping for a new jacket. He picked a plain one, practical, affordable, but he saw my hesitation and asked what I really wanted. I pointed to a teal Columbia jacket, bright and expensive, the kind all the popular girls wore. He hesitated, but only for a second.

When we got home, she exploded. "Why would you reward her like that?" she screamed. I stood in the doorway, clutching the coat that smelled of new fabric and fresh possibility, realizing even warmth could start a war.

Most nights, I retreated to my room of purple walls and turquoise furniture and sang to Christina Aguilera and Mariah Carey, the mirror doubling as both stage and therapist. My dad was trying; he was chasing Jesus, chasing healing, trying to outrun shame. But the house was heavy with unspoken things, and I wore that heaviness like a second skin.

I was ashamed of our poverty—the clutter, the smell, the peeling linoleum. Kids at school called my house a cereal box. One day, a boy prank-called just to say it out loud. I laughed into the phone to hide the sting, pretending it was funny.

Through it all, Alana and Cher remained my anchor. We were silly, dramatic, and loyal in that fierce teenage way that feels like forever. They made me believe that friendship could be holy, that God sometimes sends people before you even know you need saving.

Fridays were my favorite. Youth-group nights. The fluorescent lights of the church basement felt like heaven compared to the dim corners of our duplex. During worship, I'd close my eyes and feel something alive move through the room: the Holy Spirit, tangible and tender. Carmen, my youth leader, had a smile that felt like sunlight. She'd look me in the eye and tell me, "Tara, God loves you. I love you." And for a few hours, I believed it.

Those nights steadied me. They kept me from saying yes when temptation came packaged as acceptance, when drugs were offered, or when older boys promised attention that smelled like danger. But loneliness has a way of whispering louder than truth. And soon, another voice would enter my life, one that looked like protection but would pull me deeper into chaos.

Reflection Question: Can you remember a time in your childhood when your surroundings felt unsafe or chaotic, yet God slipped light through friendship or small joy?

Journal Prompt: Write about friends or moments that gave you belonging when you felt invisible. What might God have been revealing about His care through them?

Declaration:

I am protected by God.

I am safe in His presence.

I am not defined by neglect, rejection, or the chaos around me.

Scripture Reflection: *"So do not fear, for I am with you… I will strengthen you and help you; I will uphold you with my righteous right hand"* (Isaiah 41:10).

Even in chaotic places, God leaves markers of His presence. Sometimes protection doesn't arrive as escape, but as companionship through a friend, a shared laugh, or a small moment of joy that reminds us we are not alone. What felt ordinary then was often God quietly sustaining us, threading light through darkness and reminding us that chaos never has the final word.

Scripture Promise: *"So do not fear, for I am with you; do not be dismayed, for I am your God. I will strengthen you and help you; I will uphold you with my righteous right hand"* (Isaiah 41:10).

CHAPTER 3

THE FALSE REFUGE

The voice came dressed as friendship.

Her name was Caz. She was nineteen, magnetic, reckless, and wild in all the ways I wasn't. She wore leather and danger like perfume, and everyone in our small town knew her name. She wasn't just tough; she was one of the biggest drug dealers around, the kind of person police officers knew by first name and whispered about in parking lots.

Later, I would find out that none of my friends were even *allowed* to go to her house. Not Cher, not Alana. Their parents warned them to stay away. They said that the house was dangerous, that nothing good ever happened there. But no one said a word to me. No one told my dad. No one stood between me and that darkness. And so, Friday after Friday, he unknowingly dropped his thirteen-year-old daughter off at the place every other parent in town was afraid of.

Looking back now, I understand what I couldn't then. Being left in the care of a woman whose life revolved around chaos, cocaine, and control was not babysitting. It was exposure. It was danger disguised as protection.

We spent our nights at clubhouses—places that belonged to biker gangs, spaces that were never meant to hold a child. Their world ran on adrenaline and excess. The smell of cigarettes, gasoline, and sweat clung to everything. Music thudded through the walls even when no one was really listening, bass rattling furniture like a constant warning. The rooms were dark, smoke-filled, and lined with doors I didn't dare wonder too deeply about. I would sit quietly on cracked leather couches, sipping Smirnoff Ices, trying to be invisible while still "acting cool," as if blending in could somehow keep me safe.

Men came and went at all hours. Faces blurred by addiction, ego, and apathy. They didn't speak to me. They didn't need to. Their attention showed up in other ways: lingering glances, bodies angled too close, and eyes that tracked me from behind doorframes with a sick, predatory stillness that made my stomach twist. As the night wore on and the bikers and their groupies grew more high and drunk, the looks changed. Hunger replaced indifference. I could feel myself being assessed, measured, and noticed in ways a girl should never be noticed.

Yet somehow, I felt safe with Caz there. It was unspoken but clear. I was off-limits.

Every time a moment threatened to turn, every time a man drifted too close or let a comment slip, Caz would intervene. She always seemed to know before I did. She'd step between us without ceremony, flick her cigarette, and fix them with a glare sharp enough to cut through the smoke. No words were necessary. Whatever language she spoke in those moments, they understood. And they backed off.

I didn't realize it then, but that was God sending angels straight into enemy territory.

Sometimes angels don't look holy.
Sometimes they wear leather jackets.
Sometimes they smell like smoke.
And sometimes, they stand guard in places no child should ever have to survive.

By fifteen, the weekends had become unrecognizable. If we weren't in a nightclub, we were in someone's basement or a half-abandoned house on the edge of town, anywhere we could drink, blast music, and pretend we were free. But freedom without truth is just another kind of slavery, and I was too numb to know the difference.

The gang moved like a living organism, loud, fearless, and hungry for destruction. They called themselves family, but what they really were was a collection of orphans, each carrying their own version of pain and rage, pretending that chaos made them powerful. Wherever they went, they wrecked things—walls, cars, lives.

There were nights we'd drive to the city and sneak into nightclubs. The bouncers knew Caz; they never asked questions. I remember standing under strobe lights, my heart pounding to the rhythm of the music, watching the floor pulse with bodies and smoke, trying to disappear into the noise.

And then there were darker nights when we'd end up in strip clubs. Men with vacant eyes lined along the stage, their attention like poison. I remember staring at the women under red lights, their faces blank, their movements mechanical, and thinking, *how did I end up here?* Every beat of the music was a reminder that I didn't belong, and yet, somehow, I did.

Where were my parents? That question still echoes. Not in bitterness, but disbelief. How could I have been in those places, that young, without anyone noticing?

Caz always kept me close. She'd wrap an arm around me when someone looked too long and introduce me to people like I was her little sister, her project, her "good one."

We'd stay out until sunrise, until the streets were empty and the world was gray again. Sometimes we'd drive home in silence, the car smelling like smoke and spilled liquor. The radio would hum low, and I'd stare out the window, my reflection blending with the neon blur outside, wondering if this was all life would ever be.

Looking back, I can see it now: God's hand was in every near miss, every night that could have ended differently. Angels must have been stationed at every door, blocking what I didn't even know was coming.

But sin has gravity, and I was pulled deeper.

The night everything changed didn't arrive with a warning. It slid in quietly, disguised as just another night out, another round of bad decisions wrapped in music and smoke and the illusion that we were invincible.

The gang moved like a storm—fast, loud, and without conscience. They called themselves family, but they were more like a pack of lost kids orbiting around broken adults, trying to find belonging in destruction. Wherever they went, walls cracked, furniture overturned, and relationships detonated. It was never enough to drink or party; something always had to burn.

That night, we ended up at the edge of town in a clearing littered with rusted cars and half-frozen mud. Someone had dragged pallets into a pile and lit them on fire. The smoke rose thick into the night, curling through the air like a warning. Bottles clinked, engines revved, and laughter, sharp and slurred, cracked through the cold. I can still smell it: oil, beer, blood, and winter, the kind of smell that never really leaves you.

Caz was pacing, restless as always. She moved like someone looking for a spark, daring the night to strike a match. Trouble followed her like a shadow, and somehow, I was always standing too close when it arrived.

It never started big. It never needed to. Words would be exchanged, sharp and deliberate. Then voices rose. A shoulder would bump. A hand would shove. And suddenly, the air would change. I learned to feel it before it happened. My chest would tighten. My breath was shallow. My body would go still, as if freezing could make me disappear.

A bottle shattered against concrete. Someone screamed. Fists flew. Boots thudded against pavement. Bodies surged and scattered, adrenaline swallowing reason whole. Someone went down and didn't get back up.

I didn't scream. I didn't run. I watched. Wide-eyed. Silent. Counting exits without realizing that's what I was doing. Tracking who was closest to me. Gauging where Caz was standing. My nervous system was learning its lessons in real time: stay alert, stay small, stay alive.

This wasn't rare. This was routine.

Every weekend, there was someone Caz was hunting, someone she wanted to fight, or someone she decided needed to be taught a lesson. She kept a posse of young men around her, boys barely older than I was, already hardened by jail time and street loyalty. They followed her everywhere, in and out of trouble, waiting for her signal. If someone owed her money, looked at her wrong, or simply didn't fit into her warped sense of respect, she'd unleash them. No hesitation. No remorse.

And I would stand there, pretending this wasn't happening, pretending this was normal. My body knew better. My stomach stayed knotted. My shoulders never dropped. I learned how to be present without being seen, how to disappear while still standing in the room. Fear stopped feeling like panic and started feeling like focus. Like preparation. Like survival.

Violence no longer shocked me. It trained me. It taught me how to scan faces, read moods, and sense danger before words were ever formed. Long before I had language for it, my body was learning that chaos was predictable, that peace was temporary, and that safety was something you stayed ready to lose.

Everything slowed to silence, the way it does right before the sirens come. I remember staring at the boy on the ground, his chest not moving, his eyes open but empty, and feeling the air leave my lungs. Then came the distant wail of police radios, and I ran. I hid behind a cluster of trees, crouched in the shadows, heart pounding so hard I thought it might crack my ribs.

And that's where I prayed for the first time in years. It wasn't elegant or holy. It was desperate.
"Please, God. Please don't let him die."

As police lights painted the sky in red and blue, I stayed hidden. I knew that if I were seen, if I were linked to what had happened, my world, what little of it I had built, would collapse. Silence felt safer than truth in that moment. So I stayed still. I stayed small.

But when I finally got home, dropped off by one of Caz's posse boys who was so drunk he could barely form words, sleep refused to come. Guilt does not let you rest. It sits heavy on your chest and presses against your lungs, asking questions you don't yet have the courage to answer.

I tossed and turned, replaying the night on a loop. I imagined myself running toward the chaos instead of away from it. I pictured myself stepping into the middle of the fight, arms outstretched, screaming for it to stop. I wondered if my presence alone might have changed the outcome. I wondered why my body had frozen when every part of me knew something was wrong.

Why didn't I move?
Why didn't I speak?
Why did fear win?

At the time, I thought my paralysis was weakness. I thought it was cowardice. I didn't yet understand trauma or the way shock hijacks the nervous system. I didn't know that my body had chosen survival because it had learned long ago that survival was safer than resistance.

What I also didn't know was that something holy was stirring beneath the guilt.

Even in my confusion, even in my silence, the Lord's heart for righteousness and justice was pounding inside my chest. I could feel it, though I didn't have language for it yet. A heat. A pressure. A quiet insistence that what I had witnessed mattered, that evil was not neutral, and that silence carried weight.

That night planted something in me. A seed of holy unrest.

A refusal to accept violence as normal.

A longing for justice that would one day find its voice.

I did not act then. But I would.

Years later, that same ache would become discernment.

That same guilt would be redeemed into courage.

That same frozen moment would transform into a calling to stand, to speak, and to confront darkness with light.

What I thought was my greatest failure was actually the beginning of my awakening.

God was already at work, even while I lay awake in the dark, learning for the first time that righteousness is not passive, and justice is not optional.

And one day, I would no longer hide from the flashing lights. I would walk straight into them, carrying truth instead of fear.

Monday morning, I was pulled from class. I remember the cold linoleum under my shoes, the echo of my footsteps down the hall. The principal's office smelled like burnt coffee and disinfectant. A police officer sat across from me, eyes tired but kind, his notepad open, his pen tapping softly against the paper.

He didn't accuse me. He didn't need to.
He just said, "Tell me what happened."

For a moment, everything inside me warred: fear against conviction, loyalty against truth.
I could hear my dad's voice from years earlier, quoting Scripture I barely remembered: *The truth will set you free.*

So I told it.

All of it.

Every detail that burned my throat to say.

When I finished, the officer looked down at his notes, then up at me, and said words that changed the temperature of the room: "He's in a coma. He might not wake up."

I couldn't breathe. My body folded in on itself. I don't even remember leaving the office, just the cold air outside, the sound of my heartbeat in my ears, and the slow realization that everything I'd tried to hold together had finally come undone.

The gang turned on me within days. Caz wouldn't answer my calls. People I thought were my friends spat at me in the halls, whispering "rat" under their breath. It was like I'd been erased from their world, except for the threats that reminded me I still existed.

That night, I told my dad everything. Every secret, every fear, every sin. He listened without interrupting, his eyes wet with the kind of sorrow that can't be fixed with words. When I finished, he didn't yell. He didn't shame me. He just sat there for a long time before finally saying, "Thank God it wasn't worse. Thank God it wasn't you." It was in that moment that I knew that it very well could have been. It could have been me in the hospital bed.

A week later, I was called to testify. The courthouse smelled of paper and disinfectant. I remember the fluorescent lights flickering above me, the taste of blood and gauze in my mouth, the dull ache radiating from my jaw where all four wisdom teeth had been pulled just two days before. My face was swollen, my lips numb, but it was my heart that hurt the most. Sitting there, hands trembling, I could feel the weight of every eye in the room.

When they called my name, my dad squeezed my shoulder and whispered, "You'll be okay. Just tell the truth."

So I did. I told it all again: the fight, the chaos, the bottle, the blood. My voice cracked but didn't break. Every word cost me something; every truth spoken was another friendship lost.

When it was finally over, I walked out of the courtroom on legs that barely felt like they belonged to me. My body was upright, but something inside me was hollowed out, scraped thin by the weight of everything that had been said, everything that had been exposed.

My dad stayed behind to sign the papers. I didn't wait.

As I pushed through the heavy courthouse doors, the air in the hallway shifted. I felt it before I saw them.

Caz and her friends stood clustered near the foyer, their eyes fixed on me with a kind of hatred that was almost physical. Their faces were tight, jaws clenched, bodies rigid with restraint. It took everything inside them not to lunge, not to spit, not to say what they clearly wanted to say. The glares followed me like knives in my back as I passed.

In that moment, it became painfully clear:

I was no longer safe here.

This town had turned on me. The story had spread, twisted and poisoned, and there was no room left for healing, only judgment and vengeance disguised as loyalty. Staying would mean living under a constant threat, always watching my back, always bracing for the next attack.

Outside, my mom was waiting by the car.

Seeing her there felt surreal. She had stayed away from the courtroom, away from the mess and the public unraveling. But now she was here, steady and quiet, as if she had come to gather what remained of me before something else could take it.

She didn't ask questions. She didn't rush me. She just opened the door.

As I slid into the passenger seat, the weight of it all finally landed. My parents had started to understand the severity of what had happened. This wasn't just teenage drama. This wasn't something time would smooth over.

This was dangerous.

And we all knew it.

The engine turned over, and as we pulled away from the courthouse, I didn't look back. Not at the building. Not at the people. Not at the life I was leaving behind.

This wasn't running.

It was survival.

And it was the first unspoken agreement between all of us that something had to change.

On the drive, she stopped at a diner along the highway and came back to the car holding a Styrofoam cup filled with mashed potatoes. "You used to love these," she said, motioning me to eat them.

It was the first soft thing anyone had offered me in weeks. I tried to smile and took a small bite, letting the warmth fill my mouth. Something about it—the simple kindness, the memory of being cared for—caused my eyes to well up with tears.

The rest of the drive was quiet. The horizon stretched wide and empty, like my future, unknown, gray, and waiting. I didn't know it then, but this road was leading me into another kind of wilderness.

Reflection Question: Can you remember a time when God's protection looked nothing like you expected? When the person who showed up for you wasn't the one you thought it would be?

Journal Prompt: Write about a time you were physically weak but had to be spiritually strong. What did you learn about God's faithfulness through pain or confusion?

Declaration:

I declare that God defends me when I cannot defend myself.

I release the fear that truth will cost me everything.

The Lord is my defender, my comforter, and my healer.

Scripture Reflection: *"The Lord will fight for you; you need only to be still"* (Exodus 14:14).

God's protection does not always arrive the way we imagine. Sometimes it is loud and unmistakable, and other times it is hidden in restraint, timing, or unexpected people. When our strength is gone and our voices are thin, God steps in as defender. Stillness is not weakness; it is trust. What looks like loss or abandonment may actually be rescue unfolding beyond our awareness.

Scripture Promise: *"The Lord will fight for you; you need only to be still"* (Exodus 14:14).

Even when we are too weak to fight and too bruised to speak, God fights for us. He carries us from one chapter to the next, even when it looks like loss. What feels like abandonment can sometimes be His quiet rescue.

CHAPTER 4

THE BASEMENT

My mother crossed borders when she was twelve years old, leaving Washington for Canada at an age when roots are still meant to be forming. She stepped into adolescence carrying the weight of upheaval, into a life where scarcity pressed in from every side and religion shaped the rhythm of the household.

Faith was present—but it was rigid. God was taught as loving, yes, but distant. Not someone you could run to for help or comfort, only someone you approached for forgiveness. The emphasis was on rules, obedience, and accepting your lot in life. Sin was familiar; intimacy with God was not. Church was not a place of refuge but a place of structure and expectation, where Scripture formed boundaries more than bridges.

Her father was a farmer, a hard-working man with hands marked by the land and a past shaped by silence. He was raised in a time when origins mattered deeply, carrying the stigma of mixed beginnings and an unknown father. Though adopted and provided for, he grew up as an only child with a heaviness that never fully lifted. His parents overcompensated, and the unresolved weight of his beginnings followed him into adulthood, shaping how love and discipline were expressed.

Her mother was the youngest in her family—spoiled in her own upbringing—but adulthood hardened her. Both parents had known provision, yet tenderness was scarce. My mother and her siblings were raised to work hard, to compete for affection, to measure themselves against expectations that always seemed just out of reach. Love was conditional. Approval was earned. Children were more responsibility than delight.

This was the soil my mother grew up in.

She learned early that life required endurance, not rescue. That God was real but distant. And so, like many young girls searching for air, she rebelled early—not because she was reckless, but because she was looking for something to hold her. At thirteen, curiosity led her into experimentation—acid, pot—not as an identity, but as an escape. There were séances in the barn, not born from devotion to darkness, but from a longing for power, mystery, or meaning in a world that felt tightly controlled.

She lost her virginity young, not because she didn't value herself, but because she was reaching for tenderness in the only ways she had seen modeled. She wasn't addicted to substances in the way stories often simplify. She was a hard-working woman. What she wrestled with more deeply was the fear of losing love—of being left. It wasn't drugs that had power over her; it was attachment. The ache to be chosen.

Her story is not one of excess—it is one of hunger. Not rebellion for rebellion's sake, but a young woman trying to survive within systems that taught discipline without softness, faith without intimacy, and love without assurance.

And this—this complexity, this tension, this unfinishedness—is what shaped the mother who would one day raise me.

At the young age of eighteen, she had my sister. At twenty-four, she had me.

By the time I entered her story, she was already exhausted, driven and fiery, and completely overwhelmed, a single mother turned real estate hustler, beautiful and broken, always pushing forward as if survival itself were proof of worth, perpetually on the edge of tears. In the mornings before work, I would find her lying on the floor heater wrapped in a blanket, trying to warm herself against the cold of exhaustion, and I would crawl beside her, pressing my small body into hers, stealing both heat and closeness, learning before I had language that love meant proximity and endurance.

But as I grew older, something shifted.

Her sadness became a constant presence in our home, heavy, exhausting, and confusing, and even as a little girl, I felt responsible for it, as though it were my job to carry her emotions, to fix them, to make them stop. I would pat her back and whisper, "You're not a bad mom," until she finally exhaled and said she was okay, while something inside me quietly fractured, because it was too much for a child to hold.

Somewhere along the way, her tears stopped feeling like sadness and began to feel like control, and when I got older, they no longer moved me but infuriated me. I hardened. I built walls. I taught myself that crying was weakness, that tears were weapons, and that I would never again let anyone see me that exposed.

And that was the version of her sitting beside me in the car as we headed north.

By the time we reached the highway, the numbness had spread beyond my jaw. Outside the window, the world began to change. The farther we drove, the more winter revealed itself, leaves surrendering their colors to the wind, spinning off branches like fragments of something that used to be alive. The air carried a northern chill, sharp and honest, the kind that bites at your lungs but wakes something in you, too.

My mom talked, filling the car with noise that felt safer than silence, chatter about work, about people who had wronged her, every story edged with warning. "If you come up here and start trouble, it's not going to be good for either of us. Do you understand?"

The words settled between us like frost on glass. Why was it always my fault? Why did love always sound like an accusation? I wanted to ask her if she remembered tucking me in, if she knew how scared I was, but instead I swallowed my pride, lowered my voice, and nodded.
"Okay," I said. "I'll be better."

It wasn't agreement. It was survival.

The closer we got to town, the smaller everything seemed to become: the gas stations, the grocery store, even the light itself. The condo was beige, the siding chipped, a line of trucks sitting idle in the cold, their engines humming like a tired chorus. Inside, the walls carried the smell of cigarettes, cheap cologne, and Glade trying unsuccessfully to cover both.

She didn't have a room for me.

Instead, she cleared a corner of the unfinished basement, bare concrete floors, two shoebox-sized windows that barely let the light in, a single bulb on a chain that swung when the furnace kicked on. Old sheets hung from a line, pretending to be walls. A twin mattress lay flat on the floor beside an empty shelf.

Even my mom knew it wasn't right. The shame flickered across her face, quick and unspoken, and so she tried to make it pretty.

She took me to the hardware store, her smile too thin, her voice too bright, handing me paint swatches like a peace offering. "Pick two colors."

I chose purple and yellow, opposites that somehow made sense together. The paint went on thick and uneven, bleeding into the cracks, and as the furnace hummed its low mechanical lullaby, we stood there pretending this was enough.

That night, lying on the mattress, my breath forming small clouds above me as the bulb flickered, I whispered into the dark, "God, please see me. Please don't let me disappear here."

Weeks later, the darkness showed itself again.

And even then—even in my running, confusion, and fear—God did not leave me.

That night did not destroy me. It marked the beginning of understanding how deeply I needed a Savior.

Because even when I was running, God was already chasing me.

Reflection Question: Have you ever tried to escape danger only to find yourself more lost? How has God shown you that His pursuit never stops, even when yours does?

Journal Prompt: Write about a time when you made a decision out of fear or desperation. How has God brought healing, forgiveness, or perspective to that moment?

Declaration:

I declare that my story is redeemed.

The places I ran from are now testimonies of God's mercy. I am not defined by what I did to survive.

I am defined by what Jesus did to save me.

Scripture Reflection: *"For the Son of Man came to seek and to save the lost"* (Luke 19:10).

There are moments when we don't know what rescue looks like, only that we need it. And still, He comes. Jesus never waits for us to be clean, certain, or strong. He enters the confusion, the fear, and the running and calls us by name.

Scripture Promise: *"He reached down from on high and took hold of me; He drew me out of deep waters"* (Psalm 18:16).

CHAPTER 5
THE ILLUSION OF A FRESH START

Winter had a way of getting there first.

Winter arrived in that northern town before the calendar indicated it should, quietly crusting the inside of my window with white veins and stealing the breath from my mouth. I would watch that little cloud of air lift and vanish as if hope itself had tried to appear and then thought better of it. The hum of the furnace was the only proof that someone had remembered to pay a bill. The rest of the house spoke in the language of absence. Floors that did not creak. Cups that did not clink. A mother who was either asleep upstairs or at work for days on end, her coffee leaving a ring on the counter like a fingerprint of a ghost.

I learned to move without sound. Yesterday's jeans. A long-sleeve tee-shirt. Most mornings, I hid under a baseball cap and prayed my invisibility would arrive on time.

Outside, my little car coughed awake. The steering wheel burned with cold. I waited for the heater to find courage, watching the windshield thaw in ragged ovals that widened just enough to make the road look possible.

The drive to my new school was a measured liturgy. Fields glazed with frost, sky like a sheet of tin. I had seventeen minutes to practice forgetting. Seventeen minutes to rehearse the sentences I would not say and the ones I would. If I told myself the right story with enough conviction, maybe the day would believe me. Maybe I would too.

The school had the personality of a waiting room. Beige paint that had given up trying. Gray lockers that held secrets and the smell of damp jackets. The air tasted like pencil shavings and old fries. Behind the gym, the sweet tang of weed curled and faded as if even the smoke was worn out.

Here is the thing about invisibility. It never fully arrives. Not when you are the new girl. Not when your quietness makes other people itchy. The first looks came fast. The stories followed like birds that smelled crumbs. Where did she come from? Who is she with? Who does she think she is? Hope and humiliation moved in together and fought over the light switch.

At home, my mother and I pantomimed a life. She would pass through the kitchen with a mug, asking if my homework was done as if it mattered to either of us. I would shoulder my backpack and memorize the pattern of the linoleum. We were two citizens of a country that no longer existed, careful not to step on the borders. I lived mostly in the basement. Concrete under a thin rug. One wall was half purple, half yellow, a color decision that made sense to someone who wanted proof that darkness could be interrupted. I whispered prayers to a God who felt far away and also strangely near, like radio static that sometimes slips into a hymn. I told Him I wanted to be loved. I told Him I wanted my life to matter. The silence felt like a verdict. Sometimes silence is only the breath before an answer. I did not know that yet.

In that town, the bars did not bother to check ages with much seriousness, and the houses that held the after-parties developed their own weather. Hash burned on kitchen knives until the metal glowed and then hissed against a crumpled pop bottle. The air turned sour and sweet. Later, there was ketamine, which people called "horse tranquilizer" as if the name were a dare. Then, there were little tablets with stamped faces that sparked a promise but delivered a theft. I said no with the kind of fear that turned out to be a mercy. Anxiety carried me like an awkward angel. I watched. I learned how people vanished without leaving the room.

I slept through alarms. I skipped classes. The nightmares were a nightly broadcast. Running without moving. Voices with no faces. Hands that would not let go. Morning held a weight that pinned me to the mattress and told me it would be easier if I did not get up. Sometimes I believed it. Most times, I won.

Then there was Shannon. She was not the kind of beautiful that shouted. She was mysterious and quiet, a softness that had survived something. She kept her world close, but when she laughed, the room unclenched. Standing beside her felt like stepping into a patch of sun on a cold day. We did not trade confessions even though we silently bonded in our pain. We traded proof of presence. Sometimes presence is a confession.

The boy with the easy grin and the hockey hair found me next. Matt could drift through a hallway like he owned the idea of it. The first time he said my name, it felt like a trick. Boys like him did not choose girls like me. They borrowed them. They displayed them. They did not keep them. He kept calling anyway. He leaned against lockers and watched me like I was the most interesting channel.

Around it all, the town worked like an engine that ran on oil and boredom. Paychecks were heavy, and weekends were a storm. People drank to celebrate. They drank to forget. They drank because the sky was too big and the future felt too small. Sometimes, I could feel a pressure in the air that did not belong to the weather. It was like being watched by something that had no eyes. Tempers flared for no reason. Girls who had never met me had already decided I had taken something from them. Boys laughed with their mouths and not their eyes. Even when a day felt easy, it carried a hum under the floorboards, a sound you only notice when it stops.

I tried to make my body quiet. It refused. Heart like a hummingbird. Stomach that rolled without warning. Hands that forgot they were not supposed to sweat. I told myself this was a fresh start, and then admitted I did not believe myself. You cannot pin newness over rot and call it renovation. The truth always pulls at the corners.

Shannon and I would escape into small joys. Sneaking into bars, we knew they wouldn't look too closely at our fake IDs. Drinking Vodka Slimes until the room was spinning. Late-night drive-throughs for chicken fingers and extra salty fries, singing along to songs we pretended were about other people. We would both share a look that said, "I see you," without asking for any details. That is how girls stay alive when the ground is not dependable. They borrow steadiness from one another.

Nights stretched. The ceiling practiced its patience. I would wake with my heart running a race I had not entered. Some dreams were only reruns of what I knew. A house where the parties never ended. A couch that smelled like old breath and spilled beer. Adults who were supposed to provide safety instead created the opposite.

My father was not always the man who told me the truth and prayed over my future. He had seasons when he was swept away by his own emptiness and filled the hours with people who did not love him. On those weekends, I learned that the world can tilt. That a girl can be in a room and also outside her own skin. That some men mistake a child for a permission slip. Those memories walked beside me even when I refused to turn my head toward them. They trained my nervous system to startle at the sound of a laugh that was too loud.

Winter settled deeper.

The school day wore its uniform of routine and fear. I kept my eyes down and my back straight. Rumors still moved through the hall like smoke under a door as Matt pursued me as his girlfriend. I could not help the way my stomach flipped whenever he looked at me. I had never been the type of girl boys like him noticed. The popular ones. The golden ones. The ones with teams and fans and confidence that seemed to walk ahead of them like an announcement. When he leaned against my locker with that crooked grin, it felt like sunlight warming a place that had been cold for too long.

Part of me knew better. But another part, the younger part, the aching part, wanted to believe that being wanted by someone the whole school admired meant I might finally be safe. I thought popularity could work like a shield. If he liked me, maybe others would too. Maybe being chosen would make me untouchable in a world where I had been touchable in all the wrong ways.

He was persistent. Relentless, even. He called me from out of town while traveling for hockey and insisted he missed me and wanted to see me the moment he got back. I told myself not to be flattered, but my heart got ahead of me. It always did. I was starved for affection.

Then the rumors started. There was going to be a party. Not just any party, *the* party. The one people talk about for weeks in advance. The one where reputations are made and destroyed. The one where everyone watches everyone else and decides who matters and who does not.

I told myself I had no reason to be there. I told myself I did not like parties, that nothing good happens at them. But when Shannon asked if I wanted to go with her, I said yes before my mind could form another excuse. The truth is simple: I wanted to see Matt. I wanted to believe that maybe this time something good could happen, something normal, something girlish and uncomplicated. A boy. A party. A kiss.

I wanted one night that did not feel like survival.

But looking back, the air around that decision already carried a vibration that should have warned me. Something felt off, tugging at the edges of my peace like a child pulling a sleeve.

At the time, I did not know that the party Shannon and I were driving toward would become a dividing line in my life.

Before. And after.

Driving there with Shannon, the town seemed too quiet, as if it had stepped back to make room. Streetlights smeared gold on the wet pavement. I could hear my heartbeat in the space between songs. In the lot outside the hall, the air tasted like winter and soda. Laughter rose and fell in sudden waves. Someone held a door. The music reached me in a single punch of sound.

I stepped through the doorway, and the room turned its head. And in that instant, the story shifted its hinges.

Her name was Jodi.

Reflection Question: Have you ever stepped into something that seemed harmless on the surface but carried an uneasy feeling underneath?

Journal Prompt: Write about a time when you felt unsettled even though life looked calm from the outside. What did that tension feel like in your body, your thoughts, or your sleep?

Declaration:

I declare that every whisper of unease within me was not weakness but warning.

I now honor those signals.

I am not abandoned.

I am not blind.

God has been guarding my steps long before I knew how to speak His name.

What the enemy crafted for harm will become the doorway to my healing and my authority.

Scripture Reflection: *"I will instruct you and teach you in the way you should go; I will counsel you with my loving eye on you"* (Psalm 32:8).

That quiet unease was not fear; it was guidance. God speaks not only through words, but through awareness, tension, and restraint. When something felt off, it wasn't weakness surfacing; it was wisdom awakening. Even before you understood His voice, His eye was on you, counseling your steps and guarding your way. What felt confusing was often God gently steering you away from harm and toward truth.

Scripture Promise: *"The Lord your God goes before you and will be with you. He will never leave you nor forsake you. Do not be afraid and do not be discouraged"* (Deuteronomy 31:8).

Even in the cold mornings of confusion.

Even when silence felt like proof of being forgotten.

Even when danger hid itself behind a smile.

He was already standing between you and the darkness, preparing to expose it.

CHAPTER 6
THE ATTACK

Jodi was small, five feet, ninety pounds of sharpened edges, but she moved like a loaded threat. Hallways opened for her. Girls watched their backs. Boys mistook cruelty for charisma and smirked like they were in on the joke. She didn't survive on pain; she performed power. Two parents. Warm house. Stability. And still, she chose the darkness. Something inside me hated how people worshiped her. She reminded me of Caz without any real authority, just a bad attitude and a dirty mouth.

I hated drugs. I hated what they had done to my family. Even now, years later, my body reacts before my mind does. My heart still races when I pass a homeless man lifting a crack pipe to his lips, my grip tightening on the steering wheel, breath catching as if I'm the one about to fall apart. Addiction carved itself into my nervous system long before I had words for it.

And still, everyone wanted to party.

Get drunk. Get high. That was the language of belonging. If you showed up, you mattered. If you didn't, you faded into the background. I didn't crave the substances. I craved the sightline, the moment someone noticed

I was there. No one ever told me not to drink. No one drew a line and said, "This isn't for you; you're worth protecting." So I hovered at the edge of it all, trying on behaviors that never belonged to me, hoping they might make me visible.

The hall parties were a thing back then.

Abandoned community halls that once smelled like coffee and sugar cookies, places that had hosted bake sales, town council meetings, and polite applause, sat empty on the outskirts of town. Forgotten. Hollowed out. At some point, they became ours. A place with no adults, no rules, no witnesses.

That weekend, someone decided we were all going.

I don't remember who said it first. I just remember the pull. The quiet agreement. Cars rolled out toward the edge of town as the sun disappeared behind trees. The building loomed in the dark, its windows dim, its doors unlocked, like it had been waiting.

Inside, the lights hummed low and tired. Smoke hung heavy in the air. Bottles lined the walls. Speakers crackled with angry rap, bass thudding through a wooden floor that had once held folding chairs and children's feet. The room felt wrong, like a place that remembered what it used to be and resented what it had become.

I stepped inside anyway.

Because sometimes belonging feels louder than wisdom.
And sometimes the ache to be seen outweighs everything you already know.

At first, Jodi tried to be my friend.

She appeared in doorways and hallways as if it were accidental. Fell into step beside me. Asked questions that sounded casual but carried weight. For a moment, I let myself believe it was harmless—two girls passing the time, nothing more. I didn't interrogate it. I didn't need another thing to manage.

Then Matt's name started following me.

He was the star hockey player. Everyone knew him. His parents were wealthy, visible, and spoken about in the same breath as opportunity. In a town that fed on status, it didn't take long for word to spread that he was interested in me. That he had noticed. That he was pursuing. It didn't matter that I hadn't committed to anything, that I wanted to take it slow, that I was still deciding what I even wanted. Rumors don't wait for truth to catch up.

They just move.

And with them, Jodi changed.

One day, she was talking to me in the hallway, leaning in, smiling too widely. The next, she passed me with exaggerated sighs, eyes rolling like punctuation marks meant to land hard. Her friendliness curdled into performance. Every movement sharpened. Every look carried accusation.

I wasn't stupid. I knew exactly why she was angry.

But what unsettled me wasn't her jealousy. It was how familiar her rage felt.

She was a mirror I didn't want to look into, reflecting an anger I had buried deep inside myself. Years of swallowed words. Of fear mistaken for obedience. Of knowing when to stay quiet to stay safe. Watching her parade her resentment so loudly made something twist in me. Part of me recognized it. Part of me envied the freedom of expression, even as I rejected the cruelty of it.

Still, I didn't have it in me to engage.

By then, I had carried enough other people's emotions to know what they cost. I had survived too much chaos to take on someone else's insecurity. So I chose indifference, not because I was unaware, but because I was tired.

I told myself that if I ignored her, she would lose interest. That if I didn't respond, she would move on to someone else. That silence could still be a form of protection.

I didn't yet understand that, to someone like Jodi, silence isn't neutral.

It's a challenge.

The air smelled like rye and Coke, sweet and chemical, mixed with Pine-Sol and winter jackets bleeding in from the cold. People formed small orbits of gossip around plastic cups, laughing too loudly, leaning too close, and talking in circles like spinning created meaning. I held a red cup that wasn't even mine and pretended to sip so it looked like I belonged. Shannon stayed near; her presence steadied me the way a hand on a shoulder can steady a shaking body. Then the room changed without the DJ touching a dial.

Jodi appeared at the back doors, chin lifted, a smile like a knife. Her girls gathered to her flanks, hungry for the show. She didn't have to raise her voice for the volume to drop; attention bent toward her like iron to a magnet. When her gaze landed on me, I felt it: thin air, heavy eyes, danger.

"Well, look who finally showed up," she sang, the sugar burned black, the kind of sweetness that sticks in your throat and makes you choke.

Laughter skittered across the room, first a ripple, then a tide. I felt the heat rise in my chest, that old Caz-fire, the part of me that refused to fold. I lifted my chin.

Something in me snapped. "Got something you want to say, Jodi?"

We could have left it there.

We didn't.

The arc of her arm flashed; ice and liquor smacked my face. Cold became sting, and sting became heat. I blinked hard, and the world split into shards, and then everything rushed at me at once.

Hands. Fists. Nails.

The wooden floor thudded like a drum under boots. I heard screaming and yelling, saw mouths open and close like bad film dubbing, and over it all, I heard the sound no one warns you about: the private, hollow crack of force meeting bone. My skull. A sound you don't forget because it isn't just noise; it's a verdict.

Kicks found my ribs. My back. My face. The music didn't stop; it pounded in time with them, a bassline to the beating. The hall turned into an echo; every stomp doubled, every impact multiplied by the room itself, walls throwing violence back at us until it filled the air like weather.

I tried to cover my head. I tried to crawl. Someone laughed. Someone cried. Some part of me catalogued details my mind had no business storing: the sticky ring of rye on the floor under my palm, the scuff in the varnish near the emergency exit, and the way the string lights above us flickered like a dying pulse.

Then, clear as a bell in a storm, a boy's voice cut through.

"Run!"

Arms hooked under my shoulders and yanked me toward the side doors. The night hit me in a single, merciless breath, clean cold, honest cold, cold that told me I was still, somehow, inside this body. Gravel crunched under my boots; the sky above was a black sheet pinholed with stars that felt too innocent to witness what I was carrying.

My car door slammed. Keys fumbled. Ignition caught. I could feel my cheeks burning, feel blood in my mouth, taste iron and shame and air. My lip was split open, my eyes swelling shut as if my face were trying to protect me from the sight of myself. Every heartbeat hurt. Vision blurred at the edges like the world was tunneling.

And still, I drove.

The streets were washed in sodium light. Frost rimed the curbs. With every block, the knowing grew louder: *This is evil. This is wrong. If I go home, it will be my fault. I need someone obligated to listen.* Beneath that knowing there was a whisper, not made of my thoughts at all, a divine nudge that felt like a hand on my back: *Go to the police.*

The police station was small, the kind of place where the coffee always tastes burned, and the floors always smell like disinfectant. The bell over the door chimed when I pushed it in. An officer looked up, and the change in his face told me everything my mirrors hadn't yet.

He stood so fast his chair scraped and toppled. "Jesus," he said, breathless. "What happened to you?"

Words didn't come at first. Pain had turned language into a second horizon I couldn't reach. He led me to a chair and knelt there, eye level with the ruin of my face, voice soft in a way that made me want to crawl out of my skin and rest. "What happened to you, sweetheart?"

And then, like a machine that had seized and finally found oil, I spoke. I told him about the community hall, the angry rap, the rye and Coke, the gossip circles, the arc of the drink, the boots on wood, the sound of my skull, the screaming, and the boy who pulled me up and willed me to live. I told him because someone had to hold it with me. I told him because recording is a form of rescue. I told him because if I didn't, the night would write itself.

He listened with his whole face. His pen moved, but his eyes never left mine. Tears gathered there, not pity, but grief, the human kind that says, *I see what the world did to you, and I hate it, too.* When I finished, he nodded once, slowly, like something sacred had just been laid on an altar.

It was almost 4 a.m. when he drove me home. The cruiser heater hummed. Streetlights strobed across the dashboard. He checked on me in the rearview like he was making sure I didn't disappear between intersections. When he pulled into the condo lot, he hesitated, hand on the gearshift, eyes flicking to the front door.

"You sure someone's home?"

I nodded. It was the kind of nod you give when you're not sure of anything.

He walked me up and knocked. The door opened on my mother, hair tousled, eyes sleep-raw, surprise flaring into defense so quickly it felt rehearsed. Her gaze snagged on my face and flinched away.

"Ma'am," the officer said gently, "your daughter's been assaulted. She's lucky to be alive."

Shock, then heat. Her mouth found the shape of a question that wasn't concern but accusation, a reflex sharpened by years of her own survival.

"What happened, Tara? What did you do?"

The officer turned his head toward her, disbelief and anger threading his voice. "It wasn't her fault."

He looked back at me, nodded, gave a small benediction, and left us standing in the doorway.

Inside, the light made everything uglier. The bathroom mirror found me like a witness and refused to blink. My face was monstrous, eyes swollen nearly closed, cheeks flushed and on fire, lip burst, and hair pulled half free from its tie. I could see the places their shoes had found me; I could see the map of their hatred laid across my skin. But beneath the ruin, my eyes stared back, wide, furious, alive. I had expected to cry. I didn't. Something hardened instead, a plate cooling in a forge.

My mother's training as a medic slid into her voice, then, cool, clinical, a thin mask over a heart that she didn't know how to hand me. She decided

I didn't need the hospital. "I'll check you every four hours—pupils, orientation—and wake you if I have to."

So she did. Through that long, metallic night, she woke me by lamplight, asking my name, shining the world back into me in increments, her tenderness arriving in duty's clothing because it couldn't find any other way out. Between checks, the house breathed its usual breath: the furnace, the fridge, and the small moans of pipes in winter. I lay there on the daybed couch with the metal frame digging into my back and listened to the hiss of my breath.

I didn't pray out loud. But the prayer prayed me anyway.

I survived.

Morning didn't fix my face. It didn't fix anything. But it did something holy; a curtain lifted an inch, and the smallest line of light threaded in. I could feel the anger, the shame, and the terror that people are capable of doing exactly what they want and enjoying it.

Something had tried to end me in a room meant for community, and still, I woke. I told. I believed. And whether I could feel Him or not, God had put a hand on my shoulder and steered me toward a door with a bell that chimed and a man who cried.

I didn't have language for redemption yet.

I just had breath.

And the stubborn, quiet fact of it: I am still here.

Reflection Question: Have you ever faced a moment so violent, so unjust, that your only instinct was to survive? How might God have been guiding your hands, your words, or your steps when you thought you were alone?

Journal Prompt: Write about a time when your body carried you through what your spirit couldn't yet process. What small signs of God's protection do you see now that you couldn't see then?

Declaration:

I declare that what was meant for my destruction has become my deliverance.

The blows that sought to silence me only awakened my voice.

The darkness that tried to swallow me only revealed the One who walks with me in it.

I am not a victim of violence; I am a survivor of grace.

Scripture Reflection: *"The Lord will fight for you; you need only to be still"* (Exodus 14:14)

Evil has a sound: boots on wood, laughter in the dark, and the shatter of something that once held innocence. But the voice of God cuts through it quieter and steadier, like a breath against fire. Even when blood filled my mouth and the world spun out of focus, He was already fighting for me. His presence wasn't loud; it was the stillness that made me move. The Holy Spirit guided me through the haze and into the light of that police station door.

Scripture Promise: *"He reached down from on high and took hold of me; He drew me out of deep waters"* (Psalm 18:16).

Even in the hall where fists fell and the world went red, His hand never missed.

Even in the drive-through in the dark, His grip did not loosen.

Even in the basement, on cold concrete, His breath was near.

CHAPTER 7

PAIN RECOGNIZES ITSELF

In the days that followed, the questioning became unbearable, folding in on itself until it felt less like conversation and more like pressure. My head throbbed constantly with a deep, splitting ache that made the world feel slightly off its axis, light stinging my eyes, sound scraping against my nerves, sleep arriving only in thin, broken strips interrupted by pain and memories that refused to stay buried. My mother wanted to know everything: why this happened, who did this to me, and what I had done to deserve it, and the questions came fast and sharp, almost urgent, as if by naming the right cause she might somehow undo the effect, rewind time, or make sense of something that resisted logic entirely.

But the questions weren't really for me, not entirely, because beneath the sharpness there was fear, not panic, but recognition. And I could see it in the way her eyes kept returning to my face, tracing the swelling and the bruises, lingering on the places that spoke without sound, until somewhere in the middle of that inspection, something shifted. I felt the realization before I fully understood it: I had become her mirror, not only of what had been done to me, but of everything she herself had lived through.

For the first time, I wasn't just her daughter. I was her reflection.

She wasn't only seeing my injuries; she was seeing her life, the shape it had taken over decades. It was marked by constant abuse from boyfriends who wore her down long before they ever touched her, by verbal cruelty about her cleft palate that began in childhood and never fully stopped, mockery that trained her to believe she should be grateful for whatever affection came her way. It was marked by husbands who treated her like a doormat and eroded her sense of worth one quiet insult at a time, leaving her with a lifetime of learning how to endure instead of resist, how to accommodate instead of stand.

Now she was staring at herself through me, bruised, vulnerable, exposed, and it terrified her.

I could see the regret settling in, heavy and suffocating. The unspoken questions formed behind her eyes as she replayed moments she could no longer reach: if she had held me closer, if she had fought harder, if she had pushed past the resentment she carried when I insisted on leaving to live with my father and stepmother, a decision that had broken her heart even though I hadn't understood it then. Because what felt like survival to me had felt like abandonment to her, and the pain of that fracture had hardened into distance, into silence, into a grudge neither of us knew how to heal.

Now she was seeing the outcome of that separation.

Her tenderness felt hesitant because it was colliding with guilt, with the realization that she hadn't protected me the way she wished she could have, that she hadn't taken a stand when it mattered most, and I watched her hands hover uncertainly as if she wanted to reach out but didn't believe she had the right anymore, as if she were punishing herself in real time for every moment she couldn't undo.

And in the middle of all of that, something unexpected rose in me, not dismissal, not blame, but compassion, as I began to see her not as the woman who hadn't protected me, but as the woman who had never been protected herself, a woman whose entire life had trained her to survive rather than confront, to stay rather than fight, to endure rather than interrupt what hurt her.

Pain recognizes itself, and sometimes when it does, it doesn't know whether to reach forward or retreat.

I could feel God there, though I didn't yet have the language for it—not loud or dramatic, but present, standing quietly between us and between generations, holding space neither of us knew how to hold, as if something ancient were pausing mid-breath, suspended, waiting for a different ending.

God wasn't condemning her, and He wasn't abandoning me.

He was witnessing, marking the moment where cycles could either continue or be interrupted.

Even then, beneath the bruises and the confusion, I sensed that something was shifting, that what had been meant to silence me was being transformed into testimony, that what had passed from one generation to the next was not inevitable and not permanent.

As a mother now, I understand the weight of that moment in a way I couldn't then. I pray daily for the determination to put on the newness of Jesus, to break old habits and reflexes and ways of coping forged in pain, choosing healing over familiarity, presence over avoidance, courage over silence. Because without transformation, without the renewing of the mind, without the strength of God and the wisdom of the Spirit, this kind of pain doesn't end; it simply changes faces.

That night, my mother wasn't just looking at her daughter; she was looking at the life she had lived, and God was standing between us, quietly saying that it didn't have to go on like this.

Morning came without mercy, and when I opened my eyes, pain greeted me before thought ever had the chance to form, settling deep behind my skull and radiating outward until the world felt tilted, distorted, slightly unreal. The swelling had worsened overnight, color spreading across my face in violent, unmistakable blooms of purple and black, with sickly yellow beginning to surface at the edges, as though my body was speaking a language no one could deny or soften. One eye barely opened, the other throbbed relentlessly, and my lips were split and stiff, pulling painfully with every breath I took. When I shifted even slightly, my ribs flared in sharp protest, reminding me exactly where the kicks had landed and how little mercy there had been in any of it.

But it wasn't only my face that told the story.

Angry scratches raked upward from the base of my collarbones, climbing my neck in jagged, raw lines, red and inflamed, as if a rabid animal had clawed at me without restraint, leaving marks that burned the moment air touched them. Beneath my hair, my scalp was swollen and tender to the slightest pressure, massive goose eggs rising where my head had been kicked again and again, the swelling so deep it felt as though my skull itself had been bruised. There was no disguising any of it, no version of this that could be explained away, minimized, or misunderstood.

Standing there in front of the mirror, staring at a face that no longer looked like my own, something settled in me with a quiet, unshakeable certainty that rose beyond logic or emotion.

There was no other explanation.

Jesus had to be in this. He had to have been covering me.

With the number of blows I took to the head, with the force behind them, with the swelling that rose beneath my scalp and the trauma my body had absorbed, I should not have survived that night. I should not have woken up clear-headed enough to stand, to think, to drive myself to school, to remain conscious at all. Medically, logically, statistically, I should have died.

And yet, I didn't.

Not because I was strong, not because I was resilient, and certainly not because I was lucky, but because I was preserved.

Even then, before I understood authority, before I had language for calling, and before I knew how to recognize divine covering, Jesus was already deciding something over my life. He wasn't simply protecting me from death; He was guarding what I would one day carry. I can see it now with clarity I didn't have then: you don't survive that kind of violence without purpose attached to it, you don't walk away conscious and oriented unless heaven has already marked you, and you don't emerge with your mind intact unless something far greater than chance has intervened.

What was meant to silence me had been intercepted because my voice would be needed. What was meant to shatter me had been restrained because my mind would one day help others make sense of their own pain. What was meant to end me had been stopped because there were chains I hadn't broken yet, but I would.

That night was not just about survival. It was about assignment. My anointing. Something so divine only the Father himself can give you.

I wasn't spared so I could forget what happened, and I wasn't protected so I could disappear quietly back into life as if nothing had changed. I was preserved so I could name what happened, so I could stand in truth without shrinking, so I could live openly in a way that refused to cooperate with silence.

Behind me, my mother watched as I moved through the house, and though she didn't speak or try to stop me, I could feel the weight of everything we hadn't said hanging heavy between us. I knew she wanted to pull me close, to keep me home, to undo what could not be undone, and for the first time, I felt only compassion for the fear and regret she was carrying, too.

I grabbed my keys and left before either of us could collapse under the moment.

The drive to school felt surreal. The world outside my windshield moved forward as if nothing had cracked open, traffic lights changing, cars passing, people going about their mornings, unaware that something irrevocable had shifted inside me. My hands rested steady on the steering wheel, and whatever fear I expected to feel never arrived. In its place was something quieter, heavier, anchored deep within me.

When I parked, I sat for a moment with the engine running, breathing slowly, deliberately, fully aware of what I was about to walk into, and choosing to do it anyway.

The moment I crossed the threshold of the school, the building itself seemed to respond. Conversations died mid-sentence, lockers froze half-open, and the air tightened with recognition before the sound finally caught up. Gasps followed, sharp and involuntary. Someone whispered, "Oh my God." A binder slipped from shaking hands and cracked against the floor, and another girl turned away, covering her mouth as tears spilled through her fingers.

I walked slowly, deliberately, feeling every stare land on me like light. Shock, horror, guilt, curiosity, but beneath it all, I felt Him again, the same presence from the night before, not pushing or rushing me forward, just standing with me.

Jodi stood near her locker, unable to look at me, her hands fumbling through her bag as her friends instinctively closed ranks around her, her confidence evaporating under the weight of truth made visible. Whatever power she thought she had dissolved in the presence of exposure.

I didn't say a word because I didn't need to.

I walked past her slowly, unflinching, every bruise bearing witness, every mark speaking for itself. I wasn't there for revenge, and I wasn't there to humiliate her the way she had tried to humiliate me. I was there to expose what fear looks like when it loses its cover and to show that cruelty cannot survive once it is dragged into the light.

That day, I didn't come to learn. I came to expose evil.

And somewhere between the lockers and the stunned quiet of that hallway, I understood it fully: Jesus hadn't only stood between me and death. He was standing with me now, turning survival into authority, pain into purpose, and what was meant to end me into the beginning of my voice.

Reflection Question: Have you ever faced something that was meant to destroy you, but it ended up becoming a declaration of strength?

Journal Prompt: Write about a time when you stood up for yourself after being silenced or shamed. How did God's presence show up in your courage?

Declaration:

I am not what happened to me.

I am what God rescued in me.

Every bruise, every scar, every wound is now a story of redemption.

Scripture Reflection: *"No weapon formed against you shall prosper"* (Isaiah 54:17).

Even in the aftermath of attack, God stands as defender. He turns humiliation into testimony and pain into purpose.

Scripture Promise: *"The Lord is my strength and my shield; my heart trusts in Him, and He helps me"* (Psalm 28:7).

CHAPTER 8

GOOD NEWS & DEMONS OF LIGHT

For a little while, life pretended to be gentle with me. I had a job, a friend, a routine. Mornings came cold and dark, nights quiet and long. It wasn't peace, not really, but it was the closest thing I'd held in years, and I cupped it in both hands like a candle in the wind. I kept telling myself, *Hold still. Don't breathe too hard. Maybe it'll last.*

But in my story, calm always had an end date. And it never left softly; it tore. Except this time, what tore wasn't destruction. It was revelation.

It was summer, the kind of afternoon that made everything look softer than it really was. Light poured through the small kitchen window of my mom's house, bending through the crystal ornaments that hung on the wall. Tiny rainbows scattered across the linoleum, shimmering over the table where the three of us sat. The air was still, almost holy, as though heaven was holding its breath.

My dad leaned forward in his chair, elbows on the table, a manila envelope pressed between his palms. His voice was steady, but I could feel something trembling beneath it: nerves or excitement, maybe both. He had a look in his eyes, the same one he wore when he was about to tell the truth, no matter how hard it was to hear.

My mom stood near the counter, arms crossed, pretending to tidy dishes that didn't need tidying. She already knew what was coming. Her silence wasn't empty; it was sharp, like glass. Her love for my dad had always lived in the same room as her resentment of him, and today both sat beside her.

He took a deep breath. "Girls," he said, "I have something to tell you."

The envelope rustled between his hands. My sister and I looked at each other, her eyes suspicious, mine curious.

"Do you remember your old daycare caretaker, Lianne?" he asked.

We nodded.

"Do you remember her daughter, Danika? The little girl you used to babysit?"

Another nod.

He hesitated, then said it flatly. "She's your sister."

The room seemed to inhale. My sister froze, but I laughed. I didn't mean to; it just came out of me like a song I'd known by heart but hadn't heard in years. "What?" I said, smiling through the shock. "Are you serious? Really? She's my sister?"

My dad nodded, eyes glistening with something between relief and confusion. "I just found out. Her mom never told me. I didn't know."

I hugged him then, hard, before I even knew what I was feeling. The truth flooded me like oxygen to a place in my heart that had been starving. I didn't have to question it; I just knew. I'd always known. It was as if someone had finally given a name to an ache I'd carried my whole life.

My older sister sat still, expression flat. Her silence clashed against my joy. She muttered something under her breath, something about how typical it was of him. My mom exhaled loudly, her tone sharp but quiet. "Well, isn't that just great?" she said, sarcasm hanging heavy in the air. But I didn't care. I couldn't. The joy in me drowned everything else out.

All I could think was, *I have a little sister.*

Memories tumbled through my mind like a reel of film: babysitting the neighbor's little girl when I was twelve, her laugh like sunlight, her eyes familiar in a way I'd never understood. The way her mom would drop her off, smiling tight, the way I felt a strange pull toward her that I could never explain. That little girl was Danika. My sister. I had known her all along.

It was like God Himself leaned down and whispered, *"See? I never let you be too far apart."*

I called her that same day. My hands shook as I dialed the number. The moment she picked up, I squealed, "You're my sister!" She squealed back, and we both laughed and cried in the same breath. It was joy pure and unfiltered, like the sound of something holy being restored.

That night, after my dad left, I sat on my bed replaying it over and over, watching the rainbows on the kitchen wall dance in my mind. I thought about the years we'd lost, the birthday parties we could have shared, the Christmas mornings we could have woken up together. But more than that, I thought about the miracle of it all, that what was once secret had been brought into light.

It wasn't a coincidence. It was redemption in its simplest form.

God had taken something broken, a secret, a silence, a wound, and turned it into a revelation. He had returned to me what had been missing. He had reminded me that nothing hidden stays hidden forever when He's the author of your story.

And from that day on, I never called her "half-sister."

She was my sister.

And I was whole.

Finding my sister felt like finding sunlight after years of gray. It was the kind of miracle that made me believe maybe, just maybe, the tide had turned. God had given me something back that I didn't even know had been stolen. There were nights I'd fall asleep smiling, holding that truth like a treasure under my pillow.

But peace was always something I tried to keep alive in a world determined to snuff it out. And just as quickly as hope had bloomed, something dark began circling.

I spent my days chasing normalcy, finding ways to skip classes, and picking up shifts at Boston Pizza while I managed to pretend that what was behind me had loosened its grip. But the enemy never forgets potential. He waits for the places you still believe are safe.

The town I was living in was growing fast, with new construction, new faces, and a grocery store so shiny and modern it almost felt out of place. I had just turned seventeen when I got my job at Save-On Foods. My mom and her new friend, Carrie, were in their party-girl era: late nights, cheap wine, smoke curling through laughter that never seemed quite real. I didn't know it then, but one of those nights, over drinks and the kind of chatter that always leads to trouble, they decided to set me up with Carrie's son.

His name was Derek.

I remember the first time I saw his photo. He was holding his baby niece, smiling softly into the camera. His teeth were perfectly straight, his eyes warm and brown, his skin olive and smooth. There was something about that picture that made me stop breathing for a moment. Maybe it was the way he held that baby so carefully, protective, gentle, like family mattered to him. Like love mattered to him. I tucked the photo into the back of my math book and stared at it all the time, daydreaming about him when the lessons blurred together, and I was desperate for a reason to hope.

The day I first saw him, the snow was melting, leaving slush and puddles everywhere, that dirty kind of spring that looks like the world is trying to start over but isn't quite ready yet. I was working a shift at the store when I saw Carrie walk in with him. My stomach flipped. He was even more beautiful in person, shorter than I expected, but strong, lean, and soft-spoken. When our eyes met, something inside me knew it would change everything.

He smiled, and I swear time slowed down. It sounds ridiculous now, but in that moment, I thought maybe God was finally sending me something good. Something to make all the pain worth it.

He called me that same night. We talked for hours, his voice low and kind, and he made me laugh, not the polite laugh I gave most people, but the kind that comes from deep in your chest, the kind that makes you forget you've been through hell. He worked in the oil field, gone for a week at a time, but from that day on, he called me every night, and with each conversation, the world felt less heavy.

When he finally came home, we went to a movie, and it felt like something out of a scene I'd seen a thousand times—the shy smiles, the shared popcorn, the feeling that maybe, just maybe, I could start over. He felt like safety, like family, like love.

I fell hard. By that spring, he was all I could think about. I was still a virgin, something my mom thought was laughable. "You're still a virgin?" she had asked, half-joking, half-shocked, as if purity was a foreign language she no longer understood. But Derek made me feel seen in a way no one else ever had.

One morning, I skipped class and went to his house while his roommates were gone. The light streamed through the blinds, dust floated in the air, and the world felt strangely quiet, like it was holding its breath. That was the day I gave him what I had promised I'd save for my husband.

I gave him all of me.

For a while, it felt like a movie: the laughter, the way we'd dance around the kitchen, the long drives with the windows down and music loud enough to drown out the silence of our souls. But when I graduated and moved north to be with him, everything changed.

High Level, Alberta.

Even the name sounded like a warning. It was an oil town surrounded by Indian reserves, four hours north of anything familiar, with two banks, one grocery store, a few bars, and what was soon to be a Boston Pizza. The air smelled like diesel and wet earth. The sky was always gray.

At first, it felt like an adventure, moving in with him, playing house, believing in a future. But the cracks showed quickly. He smoked more weed than I'd ever realized, numbing himself from something I couldn't see. I started noticing how dark his world really was: the violence, the drinking, the brokenness woven into the walls of his family's home.

And then I found out he had been cheating on me.

The girl he'd been with worked at the same place I did. She hated me, made work unbearable, and glared at me from across the room like I had stolen something from her. But the truth was, they never had what we had. I knew that deep down.

When he finally admitted it after I'd confronted him over and over, my intuition screaming the truth, something inside me shattered. I had given him *everything*. My heart was raw, bruised, open. But instead of shrinking, I hardened. I got feisty. I got angry. I got strong.

I picked up two more jobs, one at Boston Pizza and another at the grocery store. I worked long hours, anything to avoid being home. Every paycheck I earned was a small act of rebellion. I started buying my own things:

shampoo that smelled like coconut, jeans that fit right, a journal to replace the one he had destroyed in one of his rages.

He hated my independence.

The stronger I became, the weaker he felt. His temper flared more often. The fights became louder, the slamming doors more frequent. Some nights, he'd be waiting for me in the dark when I came home from work, eyes red, hands twitching, his voice low and slurred. "Where were you?" he'd ask. It didn't matter that I'd just worked a twelve-hour shift. The question wasn't about curiosity. It was about control.

And then one night, it wasn't just words.

He pushed me so hard I hit the floor, air rushing out of my lungs. For a split second, I saw him clearly, not the boy I loved, but the demon that had taken him hostage. I lay there on the cold floor, staring at the pattern of the boards beneath my cheek, and I heard the voice of truth whisper, *If you stay, you will die.*

The next morning, I went to work as if nothing had happened. I smiled. I laughed. I passed out change to customers while my ribs ached beneath my uniform. But something inside me was shifting. I started putting cash aside, little bits at a time, hiding it in my purse, behind the lining, and in the pockets of coats. My friend Heather noticed the bruises, though she didn't ask. She offered me a room if I ever needed it. I told her I was fine, but we both knew I wasn't.

The night I finally left, the sky was steel gray, and the wind bit at my face as I carried a single duffel bag to my car. I packed only what mattered: a few clothes, my journal, my car keys, and a kind of courage I didn't know I had. He was out drinking with his friends. The house was quiet for once.

I stood in the doorway, my hand on the frame, and looked around at the couch where we would sit as he begged for my forgiveness again and again, the kitchen where we made dinner and plates had been smashed on the ground in his fits of rage, and the walls that had memorized our arguments. I whispered, "I'm done."

When I stepped outside, the air tasted different. Clean. Cold. Holy. I got in the car and drove straight to Heather's house, crying so hard I could barely see the road. Listening to "Foolish" by Ashanti on CD. But they weren't the same tears I'd cried before. These were tears of resurrection.

Because I knew, in the marrow of my bones, that this time I wasn't running away from something. I was running toward freedom.

Morning came like a whisper. Light seeped through Heather's lace curtains, turning the room gold and soft. For a moment, I didn't know where I was. My body braced for the familiar sounds of yelling and slamming doors, but there was only silence.

And then I remembered. I was safe.

I pulled the blanket close and began to cry, not out of fear, but release. Heather knocked gently and peeked in. "You want some coffee?" she asked. When she set the cup down beside me, she didn't pry and didn't ask questions. She just said softly, "You did the right thing."

Her words split me open. I hadn't realized how much I needed someone to say that.

I got up slowly, walked to the window, and stared at the frost lining the glass. The world outside looked frozen, lifeless, and still. But to me, it looked new. Like the earth was waiting to thaw, waiting for spring.

I looked at my reflection in the window. My eyes were puffy, my lips swollen, and my hair tangled. But behind it, I saw her. The girl I thought was gone. The fighter. The believer. The daughter of God.

I touched the glass and whispered, "You made it."

And I could almost feel Him there, not in a dramatic way, not with a voice or a flash of light, but in the warmth of the morning sun, in the taste of that bitter coffee, and in the sound of my own heartbeat, reminding me that I was still alive.

God hadn't abandoned me. He had been waiting. Waiting for me to walk out of the darkness. Waiting for me to remember who I was.

And as I stood there, I realized that was the real miracle. Not that I survived, but that I still believed I could be redeemed.

Reflection Question: Have you ever felt God stirring your strength before you had the courage to use it? What did freedom cost you, and what did it give you back?

Journal Prompt: Write about the moment you realized love was no longer safe. What was the breaking point that made you choose freedom, even when fear whispered, *Stay*?

Declaration:

I am not what was done to me.

I am what I choose to do next.

I declare that every chain of fear, control, and false love is broken in Jesus' name.

Scripture Reflection: *"The Spirit of the Lord God is upon me, because the Lord has anointed me to proclaim good news to the poor. He has sent me to bind up the brokenhearted, to proclaim freedom for the captives"* (Isaiah 61:1).

There was a time when I believed freedom was something other people experienced, people who were stronger, braver, or more spiritually "together" than I was. I didn't know that the very places I felt most broken were the places God was most intent on healing.

What I once thought disqualified me was actually the evidence of His calling. The pain wasn't random. The breaking wasn't wasted. God was already positioning me to encounter His truth, His healing, and His freedom in a way that would change everything.

Scripture Promise: *"He brought me out into a spacious place; He rescued me because He delighted in me"* (Psalm 18:19).

CHAPTER 9

THE NIGHT OF THE RECKONING

Shortly after finding refuge at Heather's, I made a decision that felt reckless to some and necessary to me. I began saving every dollar I could, not for comfort or security but for distance. When an opportunity opened up to work on cruise ships, it felt less like a job and more like a lifeline, an invitation to run as far as I could from the life I was trying to survive.

The only place I could run in the meantime was back to my mother's house, the same walls I had fought so hard to escape. She took me in without hesitation when she saw the damage, when the bruises and the exhaustion told the story before I could find the words. I promised her it would only be temporary. "Two months," I said. Just long enough to save some money and disappear again—this time onto a cruise ship, somewhere with open water and enough distance between me and the life I was trying to outrun.

Everyone knew the fastest way to make money was at the nightclub, the one the oil rig boys flooded after weeks of long, freezing days in the bush.

They came in heavy with loneliness, fueled by cocaine and alcohol, spending recklessly, numbing sorrow with noise, bodies, and excess. Money flew freely there, and desperation had its own currency.

That's how I became a beer tub girl.

The uniform was a crop top I felt humiliated wearing, exposing a chubby stomach I was taught to hide and a chest I padded with two bras to feel acceptable. A cowboy hat sat on my head, meant to complete some fantasy that had nothing to do with who I really was. It was temporary, I told myself. Mortifying. Entirely against everything I believed I was made for.

And yet, I learned how quickly I could adopt an identity that wasn't mine.

I compromised my dignity without fully realizing it, telling myself it was survival, that it was just a season. Anything to get away. Anything to run far enough that the pain might finally lose my scent.

About a month after I left, I saw him walk into the nightclub. The moment I saw him, the air shifted. It was as if every molecule in the room recognized danger before my body did. The bass thumped through the floorboards, glasses clinked, and laughter rose and fell, but all I could see was him. Derek, standing in the doorway, shoulders tight, eyes locked on me.

My hands trembled as I reached for a beer bottle, keeping myself busy—pretending not to feel the wave of fear climbing my spine as he lingered in the shadows of the club. He acted as though he wasn't watching me, though the bartender had already been drawn in by his easy dimples and soft brown eyes—wide and glassy, almost like a baby deer's, all vulnerability and quiet appeal. The fluorescent light above the beer tub flickered, casting his face in fractured flashes of shadow. In those brief illuminations, his eyes betrayed him, the innocence cracking to reveal something haunted beneath, hollowed out by rage, worn thin by regret.

He was already drunk. He hadn't come to drink. He'd come for me.

I finished my shift as quickly as I could, counting the minutes until I could disappear. When the crowd began to thin, I slipped out the back door into the frozen night, my boots crunching against snow-packed gravel. The air burned against my skin. I drove home in silence, whispering prayers under my breath that he wouldn't follow.

After leaving, there was nowhere else to go but to my mom's.

For the first time, I thought I was safe.

Then, my heart seized. A violent pounding rattled the front door.

A sound too deliberate to be imagined pulled me out of sleep. I ran downstairs, panic flooding my body, terrified my mother would wake and furious that she might. I didn't want her involved. I didn't want her afraid. I didn't want this to be one more thing I brought on to her. I reached the door before my fear could catch up to me and opened it.

Derek stood on the porch.

His breath hung in the air, thick and white against the sub-zero night. He swayed where he stood, crying, drunk, wild-eyed, desperation pouring off him in waves. The man I had escaped was now standing inches from me, uninvited, uncontained. Fear, empathy, and rage filtered through my broken heart all at the same time, making a cocktail of emotions that rattled me to my core.

I stepped outside in thin pajamas, the cold slapping my skin like a warning, like the night itself was trying to stop me. My feet burned against the frozen ground. My pulse roared in my ears. Behind me was my mother's house, warm, quiet, asleep. In front of me was everything I thought I had left behind.

I hadn't even finished healing, and already the past was knocking.

Instinct told me to run. Compassion told me to listen.

When he opened the truck door to shield me from the cold, and I felt the blast of heat from inside, my body betrayed me. I climbed in, telling myself it was safer to calm him down than to make him angrier.

"What were you wearing tonight?" he said, his voice thick with familiar judgment. "You looked like a whore."

I stared at him, confused. "Is *that* what you came here to tell me?"

With that, the brown in his eyes turned into black. Forcefully, he started the engine. The tires spun on ice. His knuckles were white on the steering wheel. I tried to speak, to reason with him, but my voice was swallowed by the roar of the truck. He shouted over me, words slurred, accusations tumbling one after another until his fury turned physical.

"Please, Derek—stop!" I screamed. "You're going to crash!" I begged, pleading for him to snap back from whatever had overtaken him.

His hands found my throat. The world narrowed to the sound of my own pulse. I could taste metal. I could smell alcohol and rage. Then a jolt—the truck crashed into the back of a parked semi truck, the impact throwing us forward. The air filled with shattered glass and steam.

I wrenched the door open and stumbled into the snow. He came after me, first behind the wheel, then on foot, chasing me through the icy dark. My breath tore through my lungs. When he slipped, I ran back to the truck, jumped into the driver's seat, locked the doors, and tore away, headlights slicing through the night.

He had been able to climb into the box of the truck. As I drove, his fists pounded the roof above my head. The sound was primal, echoing through the cab like thunder. I was shaking, terrified, but I kept driving to his mother's house, the only place that felt like might save us both.

I pulled into the driveway and rushed out of the cab. Derek had already leapt out of the box before the truck even stopped. He ran at me and slammed my head against the garage door. The metal rang like a gong.

"Carrie!" I screamed, "Carrie!"

We tumbled into the hallway, limbs tangled, rage and fear indistinguishable. I tried to climb the stairs, but he dragged me down, hands at my neck, shoving his fist into my mouth, screaming words I'll never forget: "I hate you!" "Whore!" "Slut!" "Liar!"

His mother, tiny and trembling, threw herself onto his back, clawing, sobbing, and begging him to stop.

When the flashing lights painted the snow red and blue, I sat on the steps, shaking, my breath visible in the cold. The police took Derek away. Carrie wept into her hands. By morning, there was a restraining order and a silence that felt heavier than the night before.

At work the next day, I was able to cover the bruises on my mouth, but the ones on my throat and arms had begun to darken. I made a call to my boss to find out if I could wear a long-sleeve shirt to work. He requested that I come in earlier to talk to the owner about it. The owner of the nightclub, a man connected to people I didn't ask questions about, looked at me once and turned away. Later that week, I heard he'd found Derek and broken his jaw.

It wasn't justice. It was more pain, circling back, devouring itself.

I hated it.

Deep inside me, beneath the fear and fury, lived something worse: compassion. I could still see the boy he had been, the one beaten down by life before he ever touched me. The boy had mistaken control for love and violence for power. I saw the torment he carried, the inherited curses, and the ghosts that stalked him through every drunken night.

When I heard about his broken jaw, I cried. Not because I wanted to protect him, but because I wanted him free.

He wasn't a monster; he was a mirror. A reflection of wounds that had never been healed. And maybe that's why I loved him even after the nightmare, because in him, I saw my own brokenness staring back.

A few weeks later, I boarded a plane for London with $7,000 in my pocket, a suitcase full of hope, and a body that still remembered what fear felt like. I told myself I was escaping, that salty air and distance could wash it all away. But you can't outrun trauma. It travels with you, tucked between your ribs, whispering in your sleep.

Still, as the plane lifted off the tarmac, I looked down at the frozen land below and whispered, *Thank you, God.*

Not because I was healed. But because I was still alive.

Reflection Question: When did survival stop being enough, and freedom start calling your name?

Journal Prompt: Write about the night everything almost ended. What small, holy detail—a light, a voice, or a stranger—reminded you that God had His hand on you?

Declaration:

I am not defined by what tried to destroy me.

I am defined by the One who rescued me in the middle of the storm.

Scripture Reflection: *"The Lord is near to the brokenhearted and saves the crushed in spirit"* (Psalm 34:18).

God does not wait for us to be whole before He comes near. He draws close in the very places where pain feels heaviest and hope feels thinnest. When the spirit feels crushed, His nearness becomes protection, preserving what pain tries to destroy. What breaks us does not have the final word. God does, and He stays close enough to prove it.

Scripture Promise: *"When you pass through the waters, I will be with you; and through the rivers, they shall not overwhelm you"* (Isaiah 43:2).

CHAPTER 10

THE GIRL WHO WENT TO SEA

The airport felt like another planet. Everything was too big, too loud, too alive. People moved with purpose in every direction, speaking a hundred languages, carrying lives I would never know. I stood still in the middle of it all, my hands trembling as I clutched a boarding pass to London, my entire world reduced to one overstuffed suitcase and a heart that couldn't tell if it was running toward freedom or away from pain.

My sister had told me I could do it. That I was brave enough. Strong enough. That I didn't need permission to leave. I didn't really believe her, but I wanted to. And sometimes wanting is enough to move your feet forward when faith hasn't caught up yet.

London was my first exhale. I had flown there to be trained for the cruise company that would eventually place me on my first ship, working in the spa as a massage therapist. But something unexpected happened while I was there. For the first time in my life, I realized I could be anyone I wanted to be. No one knew my story. No one knew my past. No one was watching me through the lens of who I used to be.

So I practiced confidence. I practiced poise. I watched the way the British carried themselves with quiet authority and restraint, and I mirrored it. I learned how to stand taller, speak slower, refine my movements. Inside, I was still fractured and raw, but outwardly I learned how to perform effervescence and optimism, carrying a private hunger for excellence and greatness I couldn't yet name. I knew, deep down, that this was my ticket out. My new life was waiting, and I would do whatever it took to reach it.

My heart was still broken from the chaos I had escaped. The memories hadn't disappeared. I simply learned how to push them down, to manage my thoughts by staying busy, by staying impressive, by staying ahead of the ache. Survival taught me how to perform long before healing ever found me.

Because I stood out during training, they assigned me to a brand-new ship sailing out of Alaska. That assignment would become the beginning of a four-year career on ships, a life that demanded everything from my body and very little from my heart. I worked twelve-hour days, six days a week, pushing myself past exhaustion until my muscles memorized pain as discipline.

As the days went on, I felt as though God had quietly given me a new name: capable. The Alaska air smelled like salt and pine, crisp and clean, the kind of air that makes your lungs believe in new beginnings. The water shimmered jade green beneath the summer light, and when I stood alone on the deck watching whales rise from the mist, I felt small but safe. Like no one could hurt me here.

I didn't cry. I couldn't. My heart had turned to stone, hardened by betrayal and fear, but there was peace in the distance, in the silence, in the steady hum of the ship cutting through still water.

I thought I had escaped.

What I didn't know yet was that God wasn't done with me. He wasn't chasing me down. He was patiently waiting for the moment I would finally stop running long enough to be found.

Ten months into the ship life, I applied for a position as an art auctioneer assistant. The auctioneer on the same ship was telling me I could use my sales skills for something that would pay me 100 times more in commission. He told me I would be good at it. That I was too good for the spa. Something in me recognized opportunity before I had language for it. I got the job. And there, under bright lights and fast-talking sales floors, I learned how to move people. How to read a room. How to speak confidence into hesitation. Those skills would eventually place me among the top-performing auctioneers in the company, though I didn't yet understand how much of that success was built on a nervous system trained to survive at all costs.

Working in the spa had been a ticket to survival, but when I stepped behind the podium at my first art auction, something inside me came alive. Power suits replaced uniforms. Confidence replaced fear. I was commanding rooms full of millionaires, people who'd built their lives on achievement and applause, and I realized I could do the same.

Three auctions a week. Four seminars. I sold a million dollars' worth of art every month.

Picassos, Dalis, and Chagalls were sold with a smile and a story. I was performing. I was winning. I was finally being seen.

The crew became my family. The laughter was loud, the nights were long, and the applause was constant. I used to tell my clients, "Eat a cookie, take the stairs," and they'd roar with laughter as they signed six-figure invoices like they were grocery receipts. One man bought a $250,000 Picasso, and I remember watching him sign the dotted line like it meant nothing. That was the moment I decided I would never struggle financially again.

But behind the microphone, I wasn't chasing money; I was chasing meaning. I loved the structure, the targets, the feeling of control. I didn't want the spotlight. I wanted the system. The predictability. The illusion of safety.

Then came Riley.

He was the kind of man who didn't need words to occupy a room. A gym instructor on the ships, strong and steady, grounded in a way that made you feel safe without ever trying to. His eyes were kind, familiar, almost like home.

We met just weeks into my first contract in Alaska. At the time, he was dating a woman from the spa who did facials, and most nights we'd all end up in the crew bar, laughing after long days. He'd laugh with me the way a best friend does, unguarded and easy, and even then the connection between us was unmistakable. Still, I kept my distance. I was never the kind of girl to cross that line, no matter how natural it felt to be around him.

So when an email landed in my inbox telling me he'd be joining my new ship, my chest tightened. A spark flared that I wasn't prepared for, one that both excited and frightened me. I knew something was shifting, and I wasn't sure I was ready for what that might mean.

Our first kiss was in the ship's gym after hours. The equipment gleamed under fluorescent light, and the room smelled of eucalyptus and sweat. He was closing down for the night, and I had come to meet him for a late dinner. He kissed me, soft and certain, and I felt something I hadn't felt in years: peace.

We laughed more than we talked. We never fought. It was almost too easy. We made plans and whispered promises about life after the ship. And when he got promoted and moved to another vessel, we vowed to make it work.

We were supposed to be unshakable.

Then one afternoon, I got an MSN Instant Message from Lee, Riley's friend, who was just married.

Lee: *"Hiya!"*
Me: *"Hey there! How was your wedding!? Tell me everything!"*
Lee: *"Wedd'n?????"*
Me: *"Yes! Lol."*
Lee: *"Ummmm, guess'n Riley is pulling one over on ya. He's with his girl here in Leeds. Sorry to tell ya."*

My heart sank. A heartache I wasn't ready to have.

When I confronted him, I was shaking so hard I could barely hold the phone. I screamed into the phone, "You lied to me!" I said. "You broke me!"

He didn't apologize. He didn't deny it. He just said, coldly, "Nobody talks to me like that," and hung up.

The silence that followed was unbearable. I screamed, I wept, I begged God to make sense of it. But the truth was, I had built my identity on applause and illusion. When he left, it all crumbled. For years, I couldn't shake the ache I felt for him.

Then came the call from my sister.

We were docked in Miami, the air humid and heavy, the kind that sticks to your skin. My phone rang early, too early for good news. She told me Mom was in danger again: addicted, leaving her husband, spiraling. I hadn't spoken to her in months. Anger and love warred inside me, crashing like waves. I didn't know what to do or how to feel with this information.

I hung up, walked straight to the gym, and started running. Hard. Faster. Until my body screamed and my lungs burned. I wasn't running to escape; I was trying to feel something. Trying to remember who I was beneath the performance.

Somewhere between the sweat and the silence, I knew: I couldn't do it anymore. The money, the power, the perfection—it was all killing me.

So I quit.

That afternoon, I wrote an email to headquarters letting them know I would be signing off in two weeks and to prepare my replacement.

No tears. No goodbyes. No looking back.

It was a freezing morning in Miami when I stepped off the ship for the last time. The sun was rising, but the air bit like winter. No one saw me leave, and no one cared. I rolled my suitcase down the dock, boarded a plane, and didn't even glance out the window as the coastline disappeared beneath me.

I bulldozed forward, as always, with just the echo of engines in my ears and a heart still chasing something it couldn't name.

Reflection Question: When have you mistaken performance for purpose?

Journal Prompt: Write about a time when success masked your pain. How did God use that season to reveal your true value?

Declaration:

I declare that my worth is not found in applause or achievement.

My peace is not for sale.

Scripture Reflection: *"What good is it for someone to gain the whole world, yet forfeit their soul?"* (Mark 8:36).

Power without peace is a prison. Success without surrender is hollow. But even when we run toward the world's applause, God waits, patient and unhurried, until the echo fades and we are ready to hear Him again.

Scripture Promise: *"The Lord will fight for you; you need only to be still"* (Exodus 14:14).

CHAPTER 11
THE MASK OF FREEDOM

Choosing a place to call home came surprisingly easy. By then, I wasn't attached to anything or anyone in a way that rooted me. Movement felt safer than stillness. Transience had become a form of protection. If I never stayed long enough, the past couldn't catch up to me.

I chose Canada because it was familiar but far enough to feel new. I chose Vancouver because it sat on the edge of the continent, pressed up against the ocean. The sea had become my closest companion, steady and honest, always moving forward. There was something about living near water that made breathing easier, like my nervous system trusted its rhythm more than my own.

Around that time, I reconnected with a girl named Trish on Facebook. She had been one of the few people who stood by me after the attack with Jodi. Jodi had targeted her too, occasionally turning her cruelty in Trish's direction, and that shared experience had bonded us in a quiet, unspoken way. We understood each other without needing to explain much.

When I told Trish I was moving to Vancouver, her excitement leapt off the screen. She immediately began sending me Craigslist apartment listings, convinced she was going to help me find the perfect place. She insisted on picking me up from the airport, promised to show me the city, to help me land softly.

For the first time in a long while, the idea of arriving somewhere didn't feel heavy. It felt possible. I wasn't looking for permanence or roots or answers. I just wanted space. Space to exist without explanation. Space to be unknown. Space to keep moving forward, far enough that the echoes of who I had been could finally grow quiet.

Vancouver felt like that kind of place.

My apartment was two hundred and forty square feet, barely enough space to turn around without bumping into myself, but it was mine. Every inch of it was new: new paint, new furniture, and a new beginning. The fridge was the size of a suitcase, and the dishwasher hummed as if it were afraid of being heard. The walls were a soft white, almost sterile.

I had bought everything with my own money: the crisp linens, the sleek little couch, and the matching dishes. I wanted my apartment to look like success and feel like control. My first time on land since living in survival, running from fear. For the first time, I felt like I was grounded. I wasn't just surviving. I was building something that resembled stability. But even then, the stillness scared me.

The quiet made too much room for my thoughts.

Trish and I became inseparable almost overnight.

She moved through the world like music, loud, bright, irresistible. "Effervescent" was the only word that fit her. She knew everyone worth knowing and seemed to glide effortlessly into rooms that had once intimidated me. With Trish, nothing felt off-limits. Every night held the promise of something happening.

"Relax, Tara. Have fun," she would laugh, clinking her glass against mine as a stranger leaned in to buy us shots. I had never been much of a drinker. One glass had always been enough for me. But with Trish, one turned into three, three into a blur, and suddenly the night was louder than my conscience.

The weekends began earlier and ended later. Thursday nights bled into Friday mornings. Fridays disappeared into Saturday. Sundays felt like recovery rooms for souls that had gone too far. Clubs pulsed with bass that rattled my bones. Lights flashed like permission slips. Music swallowed thought. Champagne flowed like ritual.

Trish introduced me to a world that looked like freedom but felt strangely hollow once the music stopped.

She knew all the beautiful people. The kind of people whose names carried weight in rooms I had never been invited into before. We flew to Los Angeles and Vegas like it was nothing. Playboy Mansion parties. Cabana nights. Rooftops with views that made you feel untouchable. I learned quickly how to play the part.

Mini skirts replaced suits. Six-inch heels taught me how to balance pain and poise. Nail extensions clicked against cocktail glasses. Makeup became armor. I traded the fake glasses I once wore to look smart for push-up bras and designer logos meant to signal desirability. I learned how to walk into a room and be noticed, how to smile without meaning it, how to let men project whatever fantasy they wanted onto me.

It felt powerful at first.

But underneath the sparkle, something was slipping.

I took a job back in the service industry, far below my skill level, but vibrant and fast and forgiving of excess. Late nights. Easy money. Constant noise. The kind of place where no one asks questions as long as you show up looking good and smiling. The energy was intoxicating. Beats. Champagne. Vanity. Sex in the air like currency. I didn't call it darkness then. I called it living.

Trish taught me how to be sexy, how to turn heads, how to command attention. But she also lived for the edge. On weekends, when the music got louder and the night stretched thinner, she would disappear into bathrooms or private rooms with her other girlfriends. Cocaine was their punctuation mark. Their way of pushing the night further than it was meant to go.

That was always my cue to leave.

Drugs had wrecked too much of my childhood. I couldn't pretend they didn't scare me. So I would slip out alone, heels in my hand, heart pounding, climbing into a taxi by myself. The city lights blurred past the window as the room spun. Champagne sloshed in my stomach. Anger bubbled up. Not just at her for ditching me, but at myself for staying as long as I did.

At this point in my spiral, it didn't take much to ignite my anger; alcohol was always the match. It didn't matter what we were drinking, champagne, tequila, or a bottle of wine; it all began to lead to the same eruption. My anger wasn't about the drink; it was about the emptiness, everything I hadn't said, everything I hadn't healed, and everything I still carried that no one else could see.

I would stumble into my apartment in the early hours, makeup smeared, feet aching, head pounding. The silence was deafening after all that noise. I would lie awake staring at the ceiling, vibrating inside, wondering why fun always left me feeling emptier than before.

That year became a spiral.

Not all at once. Slowly. Seductively.

I was never calm. Not once. My nervous system lived on high alert, even in moments that were supposed to be joyful. I laughed loudly and slept poorly. I skipped mornings. I numbed memories by drowning them in distraction. Pain didn't disappear. It just learned how to wait.

On the outside, I looked like I was thriving. Traveling. Partying. Surrounded by beauty and attention. On the inside, I was disassociating, fragmenting, losing track of who I was when no one was watching.

I didn't know then that I was being discipled by a counterfeit gospel. One that promised power without healing, confidence without truth, and belonging without safety. I didn't have language for spiritual warfare. I just knew that something was feeding on my exhaustion.

By the end of that year, the sparkle had worn thin.

The music still played. The lights still flashed. The parties still happened.

But I was tired in a way sleep could not fix.

And somewhere beneath the glitter and the noise, a quieter voice waited, patient, steady, calling me back to myself.

One night, we were having pre-drinks at my apartment. Trish opened a bottle of champagne that had been given to me as a gift without permission. She just popped it open like it was hers, laughing. In that moment, something in me snapped. I grabbed the bottle from her hands and hurled it across the room. It exploded against the wall in a burst of glass and foam, a violent celebration of nothing. I kept screaming and raging until everyone left. It was madness.

And worse, it was becoming *normal*.

People started to expect it from me, the outbursts, the broken things, the apologies that meant nothing because the cycle never stopped. I would wake up the next morning and stare at the wreckage, the spilled champagne, and the glass glittering like shame on the floor, and I wouldn't even know why. I couldn't name the anger, but I could feel it pulsing through me like fire under my skin.

In the loneliest moments, when the apartment went quiet and I could hear the refrigerator's hum and my heartbeat, I cried out to God. I didn't pray eloquent prayers; I just whispered His name. I begged for peace, for rest, for something that would make the ache stop. But He felt far away, like a distant memory from a life I no longer belonged to.

I remember one night at work, two girls I barely knew were talking about church. They laughed softly about their plans for the morning, about worship and coffee and seeing their friends. Something inside me ached so deeply I could barely breathe. I wanted them to ask me to come. I wanted to go. But I didn't know how to ask. I didn't know how to explain that I wanted to find God again; I just didn't have the map.

That week, I went to an Alcoholics Anonymous meeting, not because I believed I was an alcoholic, but because I didn't know where else to go. I sat in the back, arms crossed, convincing myself I was nothing like the people speaking. But as they told their stories, voices shaking, eyes wet, I felt my own walls tremble. I realized how close I was to becoming everything I swore I wouldn't.

I left before it ended, walking back into the cold night air, the city lights flickering above me. My heels clicked on the sidewalk like a metronome to my own denial. I wasn't ready to admit I was lost.

But deep down, I knew.

Reflection Question: What are the masks you've worn to hide your pain? Who do you become when anger is easier than honesty?

Journal Prompt: Write about a moment when you realized you were losing control. What was underneath your anger? What was the truth you were trying not to feel?

Declaration:

I declare that God meets me even in my fury.

My anger is not my identity; it is the sound of pain begging to be healed.

Scripture Reflection: *"The Lord is close to the brokenhearted and saves those who are crushed in spirit"* (Psalm 34:18).

Even when we can't feel Him, He is there, hovering over the chaos, waiting for the moment we stop running long enough to be found.

Scripture Promise: *"He heals the brokenhearted and binds up their wounds"* (Psalm 147:3).

CHAPTER 12

DIVINE MERCY AND SECOND CHANCES

The breakup was planned.

We'd agreed months before that if, by May 11, 2011, we still couldn't find our joy, if the laughter didn't come back, if the spark didn't return, we would walk away. When the day came, we both knew it was over.

It was heartbreak and relief in the same breath.

He was a kind man, good even, but he moved through life like a passenger: bored, predictable, and content with mediocrity. I wanted more. I wanted a future, vision, movement, adventure. He wanted quiet and sameness. The truth was, I had never really loved him. He was just safety after the storm.

Our Vancouver apartment sat on the seventeenth floor, glass on every wall, the Pacific stretching out beyond the city. In the mornings, seagulls would drift past the windows, and the mountains would glow pink under the rising sun. It was the most beautiful place I'd ever lived—sleek, new, and expensive. I could see the ocean from the couch, and at night, the city lights flickered like stars.

Leaving that apartment broke my heart more than leaving him. I didn't want to go backward. I was terrified that stepping away from that view meant stepping into the same hole I had worked so hard to claw my way out of.

When he moved out first, the silence was deafening. I stayed two more weeks, packing boxes and searching for a smaller place across the city. I remember sitting on the floor, surrounded by the echo of my own life, listening to "All By Myself" by Celine Dion and wondering how many times a person could start over before they stopped recognizing themselves.

It was ten days after the breakup when I met *him*.

The restaurant was called Cactus Club Café. It was modern and alive. The sound of clinking glasses, the scent of citrus and seared tuna, the low hum of conversation. It was spring, and the air itself seemed full of possibility.

He was sitting at a table of businessmen, the kind of group that commanded the room without trying. Cufflinks, laughter, confidence. When I was introduced, he stood up, six-foot-one, shoulders broad, a tailored baby-blue shirt stretching across his chest, a gold Rolex glinting at his wrist.

Phill Oldridge.

He was twenty-three years older than me, yet somehow, it didn't feel that way. His energy filled every corner of the room. His eyes were kind but sharp, and when he spoke, people listened. He was brilliant, one of those rare people who could control a conversation without making anyone feel small. His intelligence pulled me in immediately.

I was there on business, pitching a marketing concept to one of his friends. The meeting was supposed to be a brief, five-minute presentation, but once the wine started flowing, the conversation took a different turn.

They were planning a trip, a midlife-crisis escape, they joked, to Mexico. And by the third glass of champagne, they'd invited me to come.

At first, I laughed. *Two men twice my age in Mexico? No way.* But then Phill turned to me with a calm, disarming smile and said, "Bring a friend if it makes you feel better."

Just like that, a light bulb went off in my head: Trish. My best friend. My partner in crime. If anyone said yes to an impulsive adventure, it was her.

The morning we took off, I wore white capri pants and a baby-blue collared shirt, the same color as the sky. The plane smelled like jet fuel and leather, the engines roaring as the wheels left the ground. I remember giggling uncontrollably, champagne glass in hand, feeling like the world had opened just for me.

When we landed, the air in Mexico wrapped around us like silk—sweet, warm, and dry. The sunlight looked like diamonds scattered across the water.

The yacht we boarded was magnificent. Everything gleamed. The crew wore pressed white uniforms, the polished wood shone brightly, and the air was filled with the smell of salt and sunscreen. It felt like stepping into a dream I'd glimpsed from afar on the cruise ships.

One afternoon, we were all dancing on deck, and I put on "Bésame Mucho" by Andrea Bocelli. Phill stopped mid-laugh, listening, really listening, and from that moment on, it became our song. He made every mariachi band play it, sometimes over and over, paying them extra just to hear it again.

Later that day, Trish and Phill's friend Gary went off on a jet ski. Phill and I shared one, gliding through the turquoise water. When I leaned my head against the back of his shoulder, he placed his hand gently on my leg. His skin was warm, his scent intoxicating, not just with cologne but something natural and magnetic.

I could not get over the way he smelled. His skin, his warmth, even his breath—all of it felt like a language my body already knew. When his hand rested on my leg, it wasn't lustful; it was protective, claiming, and gentle. I felt safe, like I could hide inside that small moment forever.

From that moment, we were tethered.

The trip unfolded like a film montage.

From Mexico, we traveled up the Golden Coast to Santa Barbara and Los Angeles, wining, dining, sleeping late, ordering room service, and walking barefoot along the ocean at night. At the Ritz-Carlton, rose petals covered the bed, and jazz music played softly through the room.

Everything was laughter and heat and too much wine. It felt like a life I already knew but had never lived. I was in love, or maybe just hypnotized by my latest found freedom.

The tension between Trish and Gary grew quietly at first, like a hairline crack in glass you pretend not to see. They tried to play the part of something solid, but it never held. There was no chemistry there, not the way there was between Phill and me, effortless and electric, the kind you feel before anyone ever says a word.

Gary sensed it. The more he felt himself slipping from Trish's orbit, the louder he became. He tried to impress her with shopping sprees and overblown stories of his success, each gesture a little more desperate than the last. Trish and I would exchange glances across the room, biting back laughter, watching the performance unravel in real time. He was trying so hard to be chosen, and she was already elsewhere.

She had other men circling, too, distractions she entertained casually, almost absentmindedly, and it only fueled Gary's unraveling. One night at dinner, as Trish sat across from him, phone glowing in her hand while she texted someone else, the air tightened. You could feel it in your chest, that sharp intake before something breaks. Without warning, he slammed his fist onto the table, the sound cutting through the restaurant like a gunshot. Conversations stalled. Glasses rattled.

And then, just as abruptly, it was over.

He folded his napkin with shaking hands, tossed it onto the table, stood up, and walked out. By the time the plates were cleared, he had already packed his bags. By morning, he was gone, flying home without a backward glance.

The air was different after that. Something fragile shattered. The magic that had wrapped itself around the trip thinned, cracked, lost its hold. We both knew it, even if we didn't say it out loud. The spell had been broken. The ending had arrived.

Not long after, Trish and I boarded a plane back to Vancouver, the city waiting for us like an unanswered question. We weren't sure what we were to each other anymore. Lovers, friends, conspirators, or simply two souls running hard from the same shadows, mistaking motion for escape.

All we knew was that whatever we had been chasing had slipped through our fingers, and the road ahead was no longer glittering, just honest, uncertain, and quietly demanding to be faced.

Months passed. Gary and Phill's friendship was reduced to texts about the markets and the odd phone call about aircraft they were partnered in. In what seemed like a heartbeat, Phill and I built a life between cities: Vancouver, California, and his home on the island. We tried to sabotage what we had, yet we couldn't stay apart. The bond was magnetic and maddening. Eventually, we moved in together, acting like a couple already planning forever.

When he told me he was going to Ireland to settle family business, I was upset that he didn't plan to take me. We fought, like we always did when our fears spoke louder than our love. And the next morning, he booked me a first-class ticket.

Ireland was breathtaking. The fields glowed green even under gray skies, and his childhood stories seemed to echo every stone wall and rain-slicked lane. He showed me the graveyard where six centuries of his family rested, and I watched the reverence in his eyes as he traced the names etched into stone. It bonded us in a way nothing else had.

Then, like life always does, it shifted.

One morning, while we were laughing in a small café, his hand went to his chest. His face drained of color. The chair screeched against the floor as he slumped forward. The world stopped.

We rushed him to the hospital, sirens of the countryside howling behind us. *Quadruple bypass.* The words rang in my ears like a verdict.

We flew back to Canada immediately. I sat on that long flight, staring out the window, barely breathing, terrified he would die mid-air. When we landed, they admitted him straight into the cardiac unit and scheduled surgery for the next morning.

That night, I stayed at his mother's house. It was quiet and heavy with worry. I couldn't sleep. I couldn't eat. The thought of losing him, of losing the one person who finally saw me, felt unbearable.

At dawn, I turned on the shower. The water was warm, the light spilling through the small bathroom window golden and soft. Outside, the birds were already singing, unaware that my world was hanging in the balance.

I stepped under the stream and let the water run over me, trying to breathe, trying to make sense of it all. Then it came, this flood of words, this insistence in my chest that rose like fire. I wasn't begging. I wasn't pleading. I was declaring.

"Absolutely not," I said through the sound of the water. "You are not taking him from me. You are not taking this from me, too. You wouldn't do this to me. You will save him. You will make this okay. You will make this better. Please, God."

It wasn't polite. It wasn't quiet. It was raw, an argument and a prayer tangled together. My voice shook with defiance and faith all at once.

And then something happened. The light through the window grew so bright it looked like heaven itself had broken through. I felt it, the Presence. Stillness wrapped around me, gentle but powerful, and peace entered that little bathroom like a person stepping through the door.

It was as if God was saying, *I hear you.*

That morning was the beginning of something holy, the moment I discovered that even in my fiercest declarations, God's mercy could still find me.

When the water finally stopped and the room fell silent, I stood there trembling, aware that something inside of me had shifted.

That morning was the beginning of my return to God, not through perfection or performance, but through mercy. Pure, unearned, unstoppable mercy.

Reflection Question: Have you ever prayed from a place of defiance instead of surrender, demanding that God move, even when you didn't feel worthy of His attention? What did that moment reveal about your faith and your trust in His mercy?

Journal Prompt: Write about a time when you told God exactly what you wanted, not timidly, not politely, but boldly. What did that moment show you about the way He meets you in your humanity? Describe how His mercy found you, even when you weren't sure you deserved it.

Declaration:

I declare that God's mercy meets me exactly where I am, even in my resistance, my fear, and my frustration.

I am not disqualified by my emotions.

I am His daughter, and my voice matters to Him.

When I speak, Heaven listens.

When I cry, He moves.

When I stand in faith, even imperfectly, He meets me with perfect love.

Scripture Reflection: *"Yet I am always with You; You hold me by my right hand. You guide me with Your counsel, and afterward You will take me into glory"* (Psalm 73:23–24).

Even when our prayers sound more like demands than devotion, God listens. He isn't intimidated by our frustration, nor offended by our insistence. He sees through the storm of our words to the ache underneath, the part of us that still believes He is the only One who can make it right.

That day in the shower wasn't rebellion; it was relationship. It was a daughter remembering that her Father still holds authority over everything that breaks her heart.

Divine mercy doesn't always look like what we expect. Sometimes it's not the calm voice of comfort but the blazing Presence that meets us in our resistance, reminding us that even in our anger, we are still seen, still heard, still loved.

When I said, "You will save him," what I really said was, "I still believe You can." And that, in its rawest, most unpolished form, is faith.

Scripture Promise: *"The steadfast love of the Lord never ceases; His mercies never come to an end; they are new every morning; great is Your faithfulness"* (Lamentations 3:22–23).

CHAPTER 13

THE TRUTH THAT SET ME FREE

Phill didn't die.

That truth arrived slowly, not all at once. It came in increments. In steadier breathing. In color returning to his face. In the quiet relief of doctors' voices no longer urgent. The surgery was over, and somehow, impossibly, he was still here.

Healing took time. Three months of it. Three months of fragility, patience, and recalibration. Life moved at a different tempo then, slower and more deliberate, as if everything understood that his heart had just been held in human hands. I stayed close. I learned how to be still beside him. How to listen. How to wait.

Those months changed us.

There was a gravity in the room that hadn't been there before. Mortality had entered the conversation without asking permission. For Phill, life was no longer theoretical. Every breath felt earned. Every morning felt like grace. For me, everything was beginning. I was just stepping into my life, into motion, into possibility, while he was staring straight at the question of whether he would live long enough to see the future he was still imagining.

Somehow, we held both truths at once.

When an opportunity came to work with an auction house out of Los Angeles, traveling across the United States and hosting multiple auctions a week, it felt both exhilarating and cruel. The money was incredible. The pace was fast. The exposure was everything I had worked toward. And yet leaving his side felt like tearing something tender.

Phill was the one who pushed me forward.

He saw me clearly even when I couldn't. He told me not to shrink my life to soothe his fear. He told me to grow. To move. To operate at the level of potential he knew I carried. Loving him in that season meant trusting that encouragement, even when it scared me.

So I went.

It was a sensitive, fragile stretch of time. His life had been on the line. His heart had been opened. My life was just beginning to accelerate. We were standing on opposite edges of the same cliff, both aware of how quickly everything could change.

On my birthday, I flew to Canada to be with him. He was stronger then. More himself. There was laughter again. Ease returning in small ways. We made a promise to see each other soon, after his business trip to China, after Christmas, after the world steadied itself again.

That Christmas, my dad flew down to California to get me. We drove back together, mile by mile, crossing borders and landscapes, the road stretching long and familiar between us. It felt like a bridge between who I had been and who I was becoming. Between the life I was leaving and the one still forming.

Nothing felt simple anymore.

But Phill was alive.
And because he was, everything else was still possible.

The air was sharp and frozen that morning, the kind of cold that stung your lungs before it filled them. My dad and I were driving from California back to Canada for Christmas. The sky was gray, the roads slick, and the air smelled faintly of pine and snowmelt. Somewhere along that endless stretch of highway, we stopped at a little market called Cooper's Supermarket.

As I wandered through the aisles pretending to browse, my heart pounding as I slipped a small pink box into the basket, my dad waited by the front, humming to the radio, unaware that what I held would change my entire life.

An hour later, we stopped at a Starbucks off the side of the road. The windows were fogged, the air smelled like espresso and rain, and I carried the pregnancy test into the bathroom with trembling hands. A few minutes later, I was sitting in the passenger seat, the stick wrapped in a napkin on my lap, my breath shallow. I opened my laptop, tethered to the cafe's Wi-Fi, and opened Skype.

Phill's face flickered onto the screen. I held the test up to the camera, unable to speak. He blinked once, then leaned closer, his voice low and disbelieving. "Wait, are you pregnant?"

"Yes."

"Are you serious, babe? Really, babe? Really?"

And then the silence cracked open, and we both began to cry, half shock, half joy, and a thousand unspoken fears in between.

Nine months later, our son Cooper was born, the name we had spoken over our future long before he even existed. His arrival changed everything. The weight of him in my arms felt like purpose made flesh. Phill softened. I softened. The world grew quieter around us.

Years later came another positive test, our second pregnancy. This time, we knew what love could look like, and we were already imagining another heartbeat in our family. The miscarriage came like a storm we couldn't outrun.

Phill canceled every meeting, every flight, and every call. We curled up together on the leather sofa, curtains drawn, hot-water bottle between us, the house hushed except for our breathing. We prayed. We pleaded. We grieved.

And then, Capri.

Ten months later, she arrived, like a sunrise after an endless night. I remember sitting in the living room, her tiny body curled on my knees, the afternoon light turning gold through the blinds. She opened her eyes and looked straight into my soul, as if God Himself were saying, *This is what pure love looks like.* I felt both unworthy and reborn.

Her gaze healed something ancient in me. She was soft where I had hardened, innocent where I was guarded. I didn't know how to mother her perfectly, but I knew I would spend the rest of my life trying.

For years, I told myself I was healing. I had found a mentor who built a transformational community that promised freedom, breakthrough, and transformation. It demanded everything: long hours, deep emotional work, total immersion. We called it *processing*. I called it survival.

We were taught to scream, to purge, to face our pain until it was released. It looked powerful on the outside, with people shaking, weeping, and collapsing, but something in my spirit always felt uneasy. I couldn't name it then, but now I know it was the absence of Jesus.

This wasn't healing. It was witchcraft. It was the New Age, masquerading as light, inviting spirits to manifest, calling them "energy," "breakthrough," and "release." But they weren't angels. They were demons.

Without the name and authority of Jesus, those spirits had nowhere to go. The demons simply re-entered the individuals who had summoned them, leaving those individuals worse off than before: more tormented, more confused, and more broken. And I stayed there for years, devoted, thinking I was walking in freedom when I was actually walking in bondage.

Looking back now, I can see clearly that there was a spell over me. Not a fairy-tale spell, but a spiritual blindness. A counterfeit light that convinced me I was doing God's work when I was actually working against His Kingdom.

And then, one Sunday, it broke. Easter Sunday.

I always hated Easter Sunday. Even as a child, the story of the resurrection never sat right with me. I could believe in the cross, in the pain, in the sacrifice, but *rising from the dead?* That part felt impossible.

Decades later, sitting in the car beside Phill, our children perfectly dressed in their Sunday best as we drove to church, I was already thinking about the family photo I'd post on Facebook later. I wanted it to look perfect, our little family, radiant and polished under the bright California sun. But my heart was anything but peaceful. I kept thinking, *I just don't believe this story.*

But I wanted to.

As we turned into the church parking lot, I whispered under my breath, "If this story is real, make it real for me, God. Convict this in my heart. Make me believe."

The sanctuary was buzzing with stage lights of purple and blue, worship rising in waves. The pastor walked onstage, set his Bible down, and looked across the crowd. "This isn't going to be a normal Easter Sunday," he said quietly. "Someone in this room needs to hear this."

He paused, and his eyes found mine. "Either Jesus was who He said He was, or He was a complete lunatic. You decide."

The moment froze. It was as if every cell in my body stopped breathing. Tears welled up from a place so deep I didn't even know existed. It wasn't emotional manipulation. It was revelation. The Holy Spirit pierced my heart with the truth I had spent my entire life avoiding.

In an instant, the counterfeit light around me fractured and fell away. Whatever had held me dissolved—the spell broken, the veil torn. For the first time, I could see clearly. Not emotionally. Not intellectually. Spiritually.

That was the moment I returned—fully, finally—to the King of Kings, just as I had twenty-five years earlier in a small, quiet chapel tucked into the cold of Northern Canada. Through tears that I barely understood, with a voice trembling but resolved, I whispered, *"I believe You, Jesus."*

And He answered.

It was after that Sunday that I heard His voice clearly: *You can't participate in that community anymore.*

Everything that had once seemed so noble, so enlightened, and so empowering no longer held. The transformational community I had given years of my life to, the rooms where I had been trained, certified, elevated, and trusted to lead others, were not what they claimed to be. What I had learned to call light was missing its Source.

It wasn't freedom. It was the kingdom of darkness wearing the costume of light.

And in that moment, I knew I could never go back. Not to a community that taught transformation while denying the Transformer. Not to a system that offered a polished ninety-nine percent truth while quietly removing God from the equation.

I had spent years mastering something that almost worked. And God was about to restore what had been misaligned.

The story of my life has always been one of pursuit: pursuit of safety, of love, of identity, of meaning. For years, I chased light in all the wrong places, mistaking counterfeit freedom for true deliverance. I wanted transformation without surrender, breakthrough without obedience, purpose without submission. But when the real Light broke through, when Jesus revealed Himself not as an idea but as a person, everything changed.

This is what the truth does. It doesn't ask permission; it enters like dawn breaking through night, gentle but unstoppable. It exposes every lie that ever claimed authority and reclaims territory that was never meant to belong to darkness.

The truth doesn't just *set* you free; it *remakes* you free. It rebuilds the ruins, redefines the pain, and rewrites the story.

This chapter isn't just the story of me returning to God; it's the story of God never leaving me as He waited patiently, quietly, and powerfully for the moment I'd finally see Him for who He is.

And when I did, I didn't just find truth. I found freedom.

Transformation was never meant to come through striving or screaming or self-help. True transformation comes through the Truth, through the Word of God itself. It comes through the reckless, pursuing love of our Father in Heaven, through Jesus Christ who redeems, and through the Holy Spirit who whispers and convicts and comforts and goes ahead of us into places of darkness.

It is the Spirit who longs to speak, to guide, to be sent. It is Jesus who breaks chains. It is the Father who calls us home.

That day, the truth didn't just set me free. It remade me.

Reflection Question: When the Truth of Jesus confronts the counterfeit light of the world, it doesn't whisper; it pierces. For years, I chased freedom through performance, through self-help, and through the illusion of power. But the Truth is not found in our striving; it's found in surrender. Transformation doesn't happen through force; it happens through revelation. It happens when the Spirit of God breathes into the broken places and says, *You don't have to earn this. You only have to receive Me.*

When the light of Jesus exposed the lies I had agreed with, it didn't shame me; it set me free. He is not afraid of our confusion, our anger, or even our unbelief. He is patient. He waits for us to say, "Make this real for me."

Journal Prompt: Write a letter to God telling him what area of your faith you want expansion in. Maybe you were like me, struggling with belief in his miracle, or maybe you have a miracle you are praying for but don't have the faith to believe it could happen. Ask him to convict your heart of the truth of his goodness.

Declaration:

I declare that I am no longer bound by counterfeit light or self-reliance.

The Truth of Jesus Christ is my freedom.

I am not transformed by striving or noise, but by surrender to His Word and His Spirit.

Every false identity, every lie that once defined me, is broken in the name of Jesus.

The same power that raised Christ from the dead lives in me, refining me, restoring me, and releasing me into the fullness of His calling.

Where the Spirit of the Lord is, there is freedom, and I am free indeed.

Scripture Reflection: *"Then you will know the truth, and the truth will set you free"* (John 8:32).

Freedom is not found through striving, performance, or counterfeit light; it comes through revelation. When the Spirit of the Lord exposes what is false, truth takes its place and chains fall. God's truth does not shame us into change; it leads us into freedom by love and light.

Scripture Promise:

"Then you will know the truth, and the truth will set you free" (John 8:32).

"Now the Lord is the Spirit, and where the Spirit of the Lord is, there is freedom" (2 Corinthians 3:17).

"He brought me out into a spacious place; He rescued me because He delighted in me" (Psalm 18:19).

CHAPTER 14

THE BIRTH OF LIGHTHOUSE

It began as a vision.
It began as a commandment that God pressed so heavily on me that I had no choice but to obey. I didn't plan it; I didn't even want it at first. It wasn't a clever business move or a spiritual idea. It was a *burden*. A calling. A sacred weight that I could not ignore.

And it was *unpopular.*

When I said yes to God, the ground beneath me shifted.

The moment I turned away from the world I had built, the community I had just left turned its back on me. The warmth vanished overnight. Conversations went cold. Invitations stopped. Whispers replaced support. And then the voices grew louder.

They said I was delusional. They said I had lost my credibility.

They said I was not qualified to lead, not trained enough, not authorized to speak.

They warned me I would fail publicly, painfully, and permanently.

They told me I had no right to touch what I was about to touch.

I felt the sting of it. I would be lying if I said I didn't. Rejection always hurts when it comes from the very people who once celebrated you. But beneath the noise, beneath the fear, beneath the grief of losing what was familiar, there was something else.

A weight.

Not confusion. Not emotion. A holy, unmistakable weight.

God's voice did not shout. It did not argue. It did not defend itself against the opinions of men. It cut through everything with a clarity that stopped me in my tracks.

"Redeem My training."

The words landed in my spirit with urgency, like a command wrapped in compassion. I knew instantly this was not a suggestion, and it was not for later. It was an assignment for now.

In a single moment, I understood what He was asking. Everything I had learned in the secular transformational space carried truth. It worked. It changed lives. But it was missing the most essential thing. It was ninety-nine percent light without the Light Himself. And ninety-nine percent truth is still a lie.

Leadership without Jesus.

Healing without the cross.

Identity without surrender.

The tools were powerful, but they had been stripped of their source. Borrowed from the Kingdom, filtered through human wisdom, and disconnected from the One who authored transformation in the first place.

And God wanted it back.

Not rebranded.

Not watered down.

Restored.

I felt the urgency in my bones. This was not about building a business or protecting my reputation. This was about obedience. About timing. About Heaven reclaiming what had always belonged to it. I knew the cost immediately. Obedience would mean isolation. It would mean being misunderstood. It would mean stepping forward while others stayed silent, comfortable, and approved.

But once you hear God clearly, there is no unhearing Him.

Lighthouse Global Ekklesia was not born in a boardroom or on a stage. It was conceived in surrender, in the middle of COVID, when the world had shut down and everything familiar had gone quiet.

No crowds. No lights. No applause.

Just the glow of a ring light in a silent room. A laptop open on the table. And me, choosing obedience over safety.

There was no audience to impress. No certainty of success. Only a holy urgency to put Jesus back where He belonged.

At the center of transformation.

The first training launched in 2022. I remember opening the Zoom room, my palms slick with sweat, my heart racing. I wasn't even leading. I had hired someone else to do it, someone who had no business leading a Biblical transformation. He didn't know God. He didn't read the Bible. He didn't glorify Jesus. He was living in sin. And yet, I was paying him $5,000 a day to lead something that God had anointed *me* to lead.

I sat there quietly on mute with my notepad beside my Bible, watching him speak words that had no power, no truth, and no light. I could feel the counterfeit in the air, the hollowness of it all. I was nervous, unsure, and filled with doubt. I kept borrowing other people's belief in me because I hadn't yet believed in what God said about me.

But something was shifting.

The more I read the Word of God, the more I began to *see*. My heart softened. My eyes opened. Scripture came alive, and I finally understood that the Kingdom of Heaven wasn't a faraway place I would one day escape to; it was here, right now, available.

That revelation changed everything.

But I was still surrounded by people who didn't belong in my calling. I had placed them there out of people-pleasing, out of fear, and out of a need for acceptance. They were from the old world I had just left, the secular world of performance and manipulation. They whispered sweet nothings in my ear, pretending to protect me, while quietly draining the anointing that God had placed on my life.

They didn't know Jesus. They didn't read the Word. They lied. They prophesied falsely. They chased money, not miracles.

And one day, everything came to a breaking point.

The leader I'd hired called me, angry, his voice sharp and cold. He said, "If this is going to be a nonprofit, I'm out. If I'm not getting fifty percent of the profit share, I'm out."

Five thousand dollars a day, and still, it wasn't enough. In that moment, something broke in the spirit. It was as though heaven exhaled and said, "Enough."

The fog lifted. The confusion, the manipulation, and the false loyalties all fell away. And I heard the Lord clearly: *Let him go.* And I did.

It was immediate. Clean. Final.

I said, "Then you're out," and I meant it.

Because right then, I finally understood what God had been trying to show me all along: God didn't tell him to lead this training. God told *me* to.

This wasn't his calling. It wasn't his assignment. It was mine. And the moment I stepped fully into that truth, into the mantle God had placed on my life, everything changed.

From the moment I let him go, peace entered. The Holy Spirit filled the Zoom room, even through a computer screen. I was nervous but expectant. Unequipped, and somehow now qualified, and right before my anointed eyes, true deliverance began breaking out in the name of Jesus. People were set free from anxiety, depression, trauma, fear, shame, and addiction. Marriages were restored. Wombs were healed. Demons fled in the name of Jesus.

The training wasn't about emotional healing anymore. It was about *spiritual resurrection*. It wasn't about managing pain; it was about *freedom from bondage*. It wasn't about self; it was about *surrender*.

The transformation wasn't because of coaching. It was because of Christ.

And I knew, without a shadow of a doubt, the truth of God's promises and the identity of his people being announced really does set people free.

Reflection: There is always a moment in the call of God when obedience becomes costly. When you realize that stepping into your anointing means stepping away from everything counterfeit, every person, every comfort, and every illusion of safety that once surrounded you. I learned that obedience to God is not about being ready. It's about being *willing*.

When God stripped away the false leaders, the noise, and the confusion, He wasn't being cruel; He was being kind. He was protecting the purity of what He was birthing through me. And the moment I released control, the Holy Spirit filled the space where fear once lived.

This is what I've come to know as *divine confidence,* the peace that comes when you are finally aligned with the truth of your assignment. It is not loud. It is not boastful. It is quiet, steady, and sure. Because when God calls you, no one else's approval matters.

Journal Prompt: Where in my life have I placed the wrong people in positions of influence because I feared standing alone?

Declaration:

I am called, anointed, and appointed for such a time as this.

The vision God has placed in me will not die in the hands of fear or compromise.

I release every counterfeit alliance, every false protector, and every voice that is not aligned with Heaven.

I walk in divine authority, covered by the blood of Jesus, led by the Holy Spirit, and anchored in the Word of God.

I am the vessel He chose.

I will not shrink back.

I will not doubt.

I declare that the Kingdom of Heaven is advancing through me, around me, and because of His glory, within me.

Scripture Reflection: *"For the gifts and the calling of God are irrevocable"* (Romans 11:29).

God's calling is not revoked by fear, delay, or the cost of obedience. What He appoints, He sustains, and what He strips away is never loss but protection. When you stand willingly before Him, He establishes you and ensures the fruit of your obedience will last.

Scripture Promise

"For the gifts and the calling of God are irrevocable" (Romans 11:29).

"And the God of all grace, who called you to his eternal glory in Christ, after you have suffered a little while, will Himself restore you and make you strong, firm, and steadfast" (1 Peter 5:10).

"You did not choose Me, but I chose you and appointed you so that you might go and bear fruit, fruit that will last" (John 15:16).

CHAPTER 15

THE UPPER ROOM

The night the Zoom room changed, the light from my ring lamp felt too small for what was about to arrive. The grid of students flickered into place with faces I loved, faces I was still learning, little squares of hunger and history, while my heart beat a quiet drum in my chest. I welcomed them, set the context, and opened the Scriptures, and as I spoke, I could feel it, the air thickening as if the atmosphere had weight, as if Presence itself had leaned in to listen.

Then Jake's voice broke through, thin and trembling. "Can we stop and worship?" he asked, palm pressed to his chest, eyes shining with the kind of pressure you feel when the refiner's fire finds the places you've kept hidden. It wasn't panic; it was holy ache. The Holy Spirit nudged me so gently I could have missed it, and I reached for the song I knew He was asking for. I didn't need to introduce it. I didn't need to coach it. I just pressed play.

The first notes lifted, and I watched Jake fold forward, shoulders shaking, and the moment the melody entered the room, the pressure moved off his mind, off his back, off the armor he'd been wearing since boyhood, and I could almost see the Father wrapping him head to toe, not with explanations, but with presence. Tears came, his first, then mine, then, as if on cue, those of the whole room, because when the Holy Spirit heals one, those near the flame feel the warmth, and the hunger that brought us to this table became a chorus, quiet and electric and full of awe.

I said almost nothing. I didn't need to. In the secular rooms where I had previously sat, the trainer served as the center, the oracle, and the architect of breakthroughs, with the room revolving around their persona. But here I was only the doorkeeper. My job was to keep time with Heaven, to protect the holy hush, and to let the Spirit lead and not crowd Him with my certainty. The music carried phrases of repentance and hope.

Jake's shoulders softened. His jaw unclenched. The grid of faces blurred as everyone received whatever the Father knew they needed. I felt my cheeks go hot, my chest split open with joy, and under it all, reverence, because the King had entered and the room knew it.

When the song faded, no one spoke. We stayed in it, the quiet after rain, the clean, soft edges of a room that has been prayed in. Jake finally lifted his head, face wet, voice steady. "It's lighter," he whispered. "It's gone." We didn't ask *what*, because we could see *who*. We worshiped again, not as performance, but as agreement, and the training, this simple Zoom room, became an upper room, a place where ordinary time gives way to Kingdom time and the Spirit writes the curriculum live.

After that night, the supernatural didn't trickle; it flowed. I can't name the first deliverance because there were so many, but I'll never forget Tom. After years of secret torment, numbed by alcohol, plagued by pornography, and masked by prescriptions, when we prayed in the name of Jesus, the shame loosened its grip like old paint giving way to water. His sight wasn't fully restored that day, but it sharpened, and the man who had arrived dulled by addiction stood up clear-eyed and sober. The cravings left. The bottles gathered dust. The apps got deleted. The pills lost their argument. His church invited him to serve again, and he became a pillar in our community.

The more the Spirit moved through them, the more He refined me. He took the scaffolding I'd built to look strong: image, noise, the expensive gloss of trying to be undeniable, and He removed it without apology, like a surgeon who knows the tumor has to go. Hair extensions, gone. The high-polish marketing, gone. The personas I'd put in places they were never meant to stand, gone. Some friendships, too, fell away once I stopped trying to be manageable. Every subtraction made room for a Presence that does not share the stage. And with each layer He burned away, I didn't grow smaller. I grew true.

Scripture became bread, then breath, then bone. *Run in such a way as to win the prize. Do not be unequally yoked. I will give you the treasures of darkness and hidden riches of secret places. Forget the former things.* The parable of the talents steadied my stewardship, the parable of the sower trained my eyes to see soil, not just seed, and Paul's reminder that our wrestle is not with flesh and blood kept my hands from swinging at the wrong enemy. Above all, Jesus' Gospel of the Kingdom reordered my compass. He didn't just come to rescue us from a future hell; He brought a present Kingdom at hand. And when I aligned Lighthouse and The Academy to that truth, the room responded with healing, reconciliations, prodigals calling home, and laughter that sounded like water over stones.

We changed our language. We stripped away the self-obsessed vocabulary that promised power without surrender. We refused catharsis without Christ. We blessed tears and quiet and slowness. We kept Scripture at the center and worship near at hand. We served the widow and the orphan and the prisoner because the Kingdom is not an idea to be admired; it is a life to be lived, a table set for those who never expected an invitation.

I used to think leadership meant being unshakeable. Now I know it means holding the door open long enough for the Spirit to pass through and not rushing ahead to claim His work as mine. I used to think breakthrough was something I could manufacture with force. Now I know it is someone you make room for with reverence. The night the room changed, I learned my real job: keep the flame, guard the silence, and listen for the song He wants sung.

We closed that session the way we began it, in worship. Not loud. Not long. Just enough space for gratitude to finish its sentence. Outside, evening held the world in blue. Inside, my heart whispered the only words that still made sense: *Your Kingdom come. Your will be done. Here, Lord, here.*

Reflection Questions: Where in your life have you been trying to manufacture change instead of welcoming the One who changes everything?

Journal Prompts: Write about a time when you knew God entered a moment. Describe the atmosphere, the emotion, and the shift that took place.

Declaration:

I declare that the Spirit of God moves freely in my life.

I declare that I am a vessel, not a source.

I welcome His presence, His leading, His conviction, and His comfort.

The same Spirit who filled the Upper Room fills me.

The same power that broke chains in others will break chains in me.

I choose surrender over self.

I choose reverence over performance.

I choose truth over pretense.

Wherever He rests, I will rest.

Wherever He leads, I will follow.

Scripture Reflection: *"When the Spirit of truth comes, He will guide you into all truth"* (John 16:13).

There are moments when Heaven bends low enough for you to feel its breath, moments when God proves that transformation is not the reward of striving but the result of surrender. The Upper Room was not holy because of a song or a screen or a leader. It was holy because the Spirit chose to rest. When Presence fills a room, human effort bows. When the King steps in, burdens lift without negotiation. This is the truth the disciples learned behind locked doors and the truth we learned that night. Breakthrough is never born through brilliance. It is born through invitation.

Scripture Promise: *"And everyone was filled with awe as many wonders and signs were done"* (Acts 2:43).

This is the promise of every room God enters. Awe. Wonder. Evidence. Transformation that human hands cannot take credit for. And the same Spirit who breathed on ordinary fishermen and turned them into world changers is breathing on you.

CHAPTER 16

THE COMMANDMENT OF FREEDOM

From the age of three, I began my relationship with anger.

At first, it wasn't loud or violent or sharp. It didn't look like rage. It looked like sweetness. Like compliance. Like a quiet little girl who learned early how to read a room, how to soften her voice, how to disappear into the corners so nothing would break again. Anger didn't arrive as fire; it arrived as sadness, deep, confusing sadness that didn't know where to go and had nowhere safe to land.

As the years passed, sadness turned into fear.

Fear of being forgotten. Fear of being too much. Fear of being left. Fear sharpened my awareness and widened my eyes. I became watchful, careful, constantly scanning for shifts in tone and mood, learning how to anticipate disappointment before it arrived. Anger learned how to wait with me there, quiet but present, standing just behind the fear like a shadow.

Then fear became desperation.

Desperation to be seen. Desperation to belong. Desperation to matter. Desperation made me pliable, willing to accept things that didn't feel right if it meant staying connected. And still, anger stayed close, slowly changing shape, no longer silent, no longer hidden, beginning to harden at the edges.

By the time I reached adolescence, anger had found its voice.

It rose quickly then, easily triggered, always alert, always ready. It became protective, instinctive, reflexive. It flared when boundaries were crossed. It surfaced when vulnerability felt dangerous. It stepped in when tenderness felt too costly. Anger promised safety. Anger promised control. Anger promised that no one would get close enough to hurt me again.

And I didn't realize it then, but anger was no longer just an emotion.

It had become a presence.

Scripture tells us that our battle is not against flesh and blood, and as my discernment grew, I began to understand that anger, when nurtured, fed, and rehearsed, does not remain neutral. It becomes a foothold. A spirit that settles in the places where pain was never tended to. A force that offers protection at first, then demands allegiance.

Anger began as my shield.

But over time, it became my guard.

And eventually, it became my prison.

It distorted my perception. It trained my nervous system to live on edge. It taught my body that peace was unsafe and that softness invited attack.

It kept me vigilant, reactive, and braced, always watching my back, always prepared for threat, even in places that should have been safe.

Anger did what it always does.

It kept me alive long enough to survive. And then it refused to let me live.

By the time I came home from the cruise ships, anger was fully formed in me, not as a feeling that passed through but as a posture I lived from. It rose before thought. It tightened my jaw, flared my chest, flooded my system the moment I sensed vulnerability. It spoke for me when I didn't want to feel. It stood between me and my mother every time she cried, convincing me that her tears were dangerous, manipulative, threatening, when in reality they were simply unhealed pain echoing back to mine.

Anger had promised to protect me.
But it was costing me everything.

And this is the deception of that spirit.

It enters as defense.

It stays as identity.

And it leaves devastation in its wake.

It was only as I drew closer to Jesus, close enough for His presence to confront what I had mistaken for strength, that the anger began to feel foreign, heavy, incompatible with the peace my soul was tasting. The rage that once felt necessary began to feel toxic, like something my body could no longer carry without consequence.

For the first time, I could see it clearly.

Anger was not who I was.

It was what I had learned.

And once it was named, once it was brought into the light, it could no longer rule me.

Because spirits lose authority when truth is spoken. And what is exposed no longer gets to stay.

I would feel it first in my temples, a sudden tightening, pressure building until my jaw locked and my vision sharpened, and then it would drop straight into my chest, hot and immediate, demanding release, because anger was the language my body had learned long before my mind ever understood it.

Once triggered, I could explode without warning. I was twenty-three when my mother became sober. Looking back, this seemed to be my free pass to release years of unresolved pain, reaching for every wound, every abandonment, every childhood memory, and turning them into ammunition. It was telling her to shut up, telling her to stop crying, telling her exactly how she had failed me, unaware that none of my words were actually aimed at her. Every accusation was really directed at my own unhealed pain, the pain of a little girl who had never been comforted and who had always been the comforter, the child who learned early that survival meant staying alert, staying strong, and staying armored. At first, I felt nothing but the rage within me. Justified in eruption. "She deserved it," I would say when guilt would try to knock.

It wasn't until I had my own children and began transforming that I saw her differently.

I now looked at my mother; I could see the pain in her eyes, and it startled me how solid it looked: regret, shame, and guilt layered so densely they felt almost physical, as if they carried weight and texture, as if they pressed outward from behind her face. And as my discernment began to sharpen, I started noticing something else beneath it all, something heavier than emotion, something oppressive that seemed to cling close to her, feeding on accusation and agreement, growing louder every time I erupted. I didn't have language for it yet, only the unsettling awareness that my anger wasn't neutral, that I was feeding something dark even as I believed I was protecting myself.

Anger had always felt safer than softness.

Vulnerability, crying, openness: those things felt too risky, too exposed. Anger gave me edges. It gave me distance. It gave me control over the environment. It was how I made sure nothing could sneak up on me from behind, how I kept threats visible and manageable, how I stayed alive. Long before I knew words like "trauma" or "neural pathways," my nervous system had learned to live braced, scanning, vigilant, because when danger comes early, vigilance becomes home.

But there comes a point in healing where anger can no longer survive.

The closer I drew to Jesus, the softer my heart became, and the rage that once felt powerful began to feel foreign, like poison I could no longer stomach. What had once felt like armor started to feel like weight. The anger that had given me clarity began to blur my vision. And one day, without planning to, I cried again, not out of fury or protest but out of grief.

I found myself looking at my mother and seeing her, not as the villain in my story but as the broken girl in hers, finally able to recognize how much she had lost, how much pain she had carried, how much of herself she had given away just to survive. She wasn't the enemy. She was a wounded woman who had done her best without ever being shown how to heal. And when the thought landed in me: *She's just a shell of who she was meant to be*, it didn't ignite anger. It broke my heart. For the first time, I could see her through the eyes of Christ, through the eyes of mercy.

It was May in Southern California, sunlight pouring down warm and golden, when God gave me the opportunity to make it right. We sat in my brand-new Range Rover, toddler seats buckled in the back for our four- and two-year-old, the saddle-brown interior glowing against the gray-bronze exterior that shimmered in the light, parked quietly on a residential street while my mother cried again, but this time she wasn't defensive or controlling. She looked defeated. Emptied. Like someone who had finally run out of ways to protect herself.

And I realized I could no longer carry the anger.

Not another mile. Not another minute.

I pulled into my driveway. Reached over gently for her hand and told her that I loved her, that I was sorry, not vaguely or spiritually but specifically for being dishonoring, judgmental, and cruel, for carrying darkness in my heart and mistaking it for strength. I told her she could count on me to honor her, to hold her high, to speak life over her from that day forward.

The atmosphere shifted instantly.

Her body went limp, her shoulders dropped, and the tears that fell were not the familiar ones I had grown up with, but tears of freedom, as she began to shake and sob while the Spirit of God filled that car. I watched something lift, something loosen its grip, something retreat, and though I didn't have language for it then, I understand now that what I witnessed was deliverance through the power of forgiveness. She looked light, deflated of years of heaviness, her eyes clear, her face peaceful, and for the first time in my life, I saw my mother's true face, the one God had made before the world broke her.

"Forgiveness" is one of those words that carries a charge long before we ever define it.

For many people, just hearing it tightens the chest, summons faces that never apologized, wounds that were never acknowledged, injustices that still feel unresolved. The word drags behind it a thousand questions. *What if they don't accept it? What if they never change? What if forgiving means excusing? What if it means forgetting? What if I go first and I'm exposed again? What if they were supposed to ask me?*

So much lives inside that single word.

I realized I had always treated forgiveness as an emotional event, something to feel my way into, something dependent on timing or apology or outcome. But Scripture never framed it that way. Jesus spoke of forgiveness as release. *Loosen what is bound.* Paul wrote of being transformed by the renewing of the mind. And slowly, I began to understand that forgiveness was not about them at all. It was about interrupting old agreements, cutting cords I didn't even know were attached, retraining a mind that had learned to defend its belief systems at all costs.

Neuroscience calls it survival circuitry. Psychology calls it a defense mechanism. Scripture calls it the old mind, the one that must be renewed. All three were telling the same story: my anger wasn't proof I was broken; it was proof I had adapted. But what once protected me was now costing me intimacy, costing me peace, and costing me the very tenderness I longed to give my children.

The brain protects what it believes keeps it alive.

Until we tell it no.

So I began using forgiveness that way, not ceremonially, not emotionally, not dramatically, but deliberately, repeatedly, every time resentment surfaced, every time memory tightened my chest, and every time anger rose to protect me. Forgiveness became a tool, a blade that severed old ties, a way of telling my body, *You are safe now.* And something extraordinary happened. My inner world grew quieter. My reactions softened. My relationships became cleaner. Peace stopped feeling fragile.

The miracle of forgiveness is that it is designed to bless you in a full circle. A year later, my mother went through healing and transformational work, and while she was in her process, we spoke:

"Mom, you don't have to do this. I forgive you," I said to her at the beginning of the call. I did everything I could to not bring up the wounds of my heart, wanting to avoid vulnerability and intimacy at all costs.

"Please. Let me do this. You did this for me last year, and I want to give this to you."

I obliged.

We wept together for two straight hours. She owned and apologized for every way she had hurt me, abandoned me, and failed to protect me, telling me she wished she could go back and do it all over again, admitting she had been lost and broken. Diving generously into memories neither one of us could bear to taste again. But she did it anyway. Owning it all. One hundred percent responsible.

Her words healed something deep in me that I hadn't known was still wounded, and still, to this day, those are the two conversations that restored everything.

Today, my mom is radiant, filled with faith and expectancy for miracles, walking in humility, grace, and strength, praying for me, laughing again, and somehow becoming my best friend.

My father's redemption came differently. He carried his love for Christ his entire life, even though he never fully broke free from the chains of unworthiness placed on him, spending thirty-five years in a sawmill, day after day, shift after shift, until he finally retired, and exactly one year later, that same sawmill burned to the ground, killing the man who took his place.

God spared him.

My dad was the kindest man I knew, gentle and patient, never harsh in discipline, always encouraging, telling me to tell the truth, to go the extra mile, that a job worth doing was a job worth doing well, caring more about character than report cards, teaching me Philippians 4:8, and showing me by example how to fix my mind on what was pure and good. When I look at him now, I see a man imprisoned by his own mind yet determined to make sure I was free.

And that is why the fifth commandment, "Honor your father and mother," means something entirely different to me now. For years, I thought it was cruel, a demand to give honor to people who hadn't earned it, but I've come to understand that honor is not a gift to them. It is freedom for you.

Honor releases heaven's power. It is the bridge between generational bondage and generational blessing. It sets you free. Because forgiveness is not agreement with the pain. It is the release of it into the hands of the only One who can redeem it.

And in the Kingdom, forgiveness is warfare.

Reflection Question: Ask yourself: *Who have I been blaming for my pain? Where have I allowed anger to protect me from love? Whose tears have I hardened my heart against? What would it look like to forgive, not for them, but for you?*

Journal Prompt: Write a letter to your mother or father, or both. Thank them for what they did right. Forgive them for what they didn't know how to do. Ask the Holy Spirit to show you how *they* were once little children who were never held, never seen, and never told who they were in Christ. Then bless them. Speak life over them.

Declaration:

I am free from the inheritance of pain.

I walk in compassion and truth.

The same grace that saved me covers my parents.

I honor them, not because of who they were, but because of who God is in me.

I choose mercy over memory.

I choose blessing over bitterness.

I choose freedom over fear.

Scripture Reflection: *"I will restore to you the years that the locust has eaten"* (Joel 2:25).

God's promise of restoration reaches further than our memories and deeper than our wounds. He is not limited by what was lost, mishandled, or broken in past generations. What pain consumed, God can redeem. Forgiveness does not erase the past, but it releases us from carrying it forward. When we choose mercy, God restores what bitterness could never heal.

Scripture Promise: *"I will restore to you the years that the locust has eaten"* (Joel 2:25).

CHAPTER 17

REDEEMING THE GROUND

When God began showing me how psychology had replaced deliverance, He also began exposing the system I had once been a part of in the secular transformational world. What I thought was personal development and healing was actually a demonic counterfeit, a training ground of false light, false idols, and false healing.

It was the language of the work that first seduced me: *transformation, authenticity, breakthrough*. It all sounded so good. So close to the truth.

But the Lord began whispering to me, *"No one lights a lamp and hides it under a container"* (Luke 8:16).

It struck me like a lightning bolt because that's exactly what was happening: light was being hidden under darkness and renamed as illumination. The "container" wasn't holding light; it was *covering* it.

Inside those training rooms, everything looked powerful on the surface, with people crying, confessing, screaming, and shaking. They called it a "breakthrough," but the Holy Spirit was not a part of it. I now understand it for what it was: a counterfeit deliverance. The enemy had created a mockery of transformation, an imitation that looked like freedom but left people more bound than before.

They called it "energetic release." I now know it was *a demonic manifestation.*

They called it "emotional clearing." I now know it was *soulish catharsis.*

They called it "activation." I now know it was *possession.*

Because without Jesus, there is no deliverance. Without the name above every name, every "breakthrough" becomes another open door.

The Bible says, *"When an unclean spirit goes out of a man, it passes through arid places seeking rest and finds none. Then it says, 'I will return to the house I left.' When it arrives, it finds the house swept clean but unoccupied. Then it goes and takes seven other spirits more wicked than itself, and they go in and dwell there"* (Luke 11:24–26).

That's what those containers were doing. They were emptying people of pain but not filling them with truth. They were opening the soul but not sealing it with the Spirit.

I remember sitting in those rooms, watching people writhe and weep on the floor, thinking they were being "set free," when in reality they were just being emptied and left vulnerable. And I was a part of it. I was teaching inside it. I was leading others into it. The deception was thick, like honey laced with poison. It felt sweet. It looked sincere. But it was death dressed as light. The Bible says, *"Even Satan disguises himself as an angel of light"* (2 Corinthians 11:14).

It wasn't until God began softening my heart and showing me His true spirit of peace and holiness that I began to feel the dissonance in my soul. Something in me started to recoil. The very atmosphere that had once felt empowering now felt heavy and oppressive. I would leave those weekends feeling sick, not just physically, but spiritually. My body would shake, my dreams would be dark, and the Lord began convicting me.

One night after a training, I remember being alone in my car, sobbing, and hearing the voice of God so clearly say, *Daughter, you've been building altars to freedom that don't have My fire.*

I froze. I knew exactly what He meant. I was offering transformation without the Transformer. Healing without the Healer. Light without the Lampstand. Truth without the Word. And then He said something that changed everything: *Redeem it.*

I didn't know what that meant at first. Redeem what? Redeem them? Redeem the people? Redeem the method? But He clarified: *Redeem the ground. What the enemy has used to counterfeit My glory, you will reclaim for My Kingdom.*

I realized then that the enemy doesn't create; he only counterfeits. He mimics what already exists in Heaven and distorts it with pride, control, and self-worship. The "training room" was a stolen blueprint. It was God's design for transformation, without His Spirit.

God's Spirit had shown me true deliverance. He had shown me the real power of repentance, confession, and renewal. He had shown me what happens when light invades darkness: people don't just scream; they are *set free.*

And I knew from that moment forward that He was calling me to rebuild what the enemy had perverted, to create a Kingdom training ground where transformation wasn't emotional manipulation but a holy encounter.

That's how Lighthouse was born. Not as a business plan. Not as a coaching company. But as an act of holy redemption.

I had seen the counterfeit. Now I was carrying the real thing.

In the months that followed, God began showing me just how deep the world's deception runs. The very foundation of modern culture is built on one dangerous idol: the self. *Self-love. Self-worth. Self-healing. Self-discipline. Self-awareness.* It sounds harmless, even healthy, but it's a slow poison that's crippled a generation.

Because here's the truth: you cannot "self" your way to salvation. The more we glorify self, the further we drift from surrender. And the more we worship self, the less room we give the Spirit.

The Bible says, *"If anyone wishes to come after Me, he must deny himself, take up his cross daily, and follow Me"* (Luke 9:23). While the world says, "Follow your heart," Jesus says, *"The heart is deceitful above all things"* (Jeremiah 17:9).

We've been tricked into thinking that healing is something we do for ourselves, when it's actually something God does *in us*. We've traded repentance for self-regulation, deliverance for dopamine, and intimacy for independence. It's the oldest lie in the book: *"You will be like God"* (Genesis 3:5).

The self-help movement isn't new. It's just the Garden of Eden repackaged with better lighting. And yet, it's everywhere, with gurus, influencers, and mentors all preaching that you are your own savior. But the Bible says the exact opposite: *"Apart from Me, you can do nothing"* (John 15:5).

That's why the "self" movement feels so exhausting. Because it is. It's a treadmill with no finish line, a constant pursuit of fixing something that only surrender can heal.

True transformation doesn't come through affirmation. It comes through repentance. It doesn't come through self-help. It comes through *Spirit-help*. It doesn't come from striving to become more. It comes from dying to self so that Christ can live through us.

This is why the world is more anxious, more depressed, and more lost than ever. It's chasing peace that can't be purchased, purpose that can't be manufactured, and identity that can't be found outside of Jesus.

The Lord said to me one morning as I prayed over the curriculum for Lighthouse: *The greatest counterfeit the enemy ever built was self-sufficiency.* The very place we were taught to find freedom, in ourselves, is the place we became most enslaved.

Reflection: There is a moment in every believer's journey when the Holy Spirit gently asks a question that shakes the foundations upon which we have built our lives. This is one of those moments.

The world tells us that hope can be found in effort. In strategy. In systems. In experts who promise answers for every ache of the human soul.

But none of it lasts. None of it speaks in the quiet. None of it holds when the night comes.

We chase voices that promise clarity and end up more confused. We follow people who promise healing and end up more fractured. We bow to teachings that glitter with wisdom but leave us thirsty for the living water we were made for.

Hope that must be maintained by human strength will eventually fail.

There is only One whose voice steadies storms. Only One who brings peace that does not depend on circumstance. Only One whose truth does not shift with culture. Only One who knows how to reach the deep places you do not speak of.

His name is Jesus.

He does not sell you peace. He is your peace. He does not ask you to find your own truth. He is the Truth. He does not demand perfection. He asks for surrender.

Every longing in you is proof that the world cannot fulfill what Heaven created. Every ache inside you is an invitation to return. Every unanswered prayer is a reminder that silence is not absence. He is closer than your breath, waiting for the moment you stop striving long enough to hear Him whisper.

Let this be that moment. Slow down. Let your shoulders fall. Let your heart exhale. Let the Presence of God meet you in the place where your strength ends and His begins.

You do not need to perform for Him. You do not need to impress Him. You only need to open your hands.

He is here. He always has been.

Reflection Questions: Where have you been placing your hope in something other than Jesus?

Journal Prompt: Write honestly about the places where you have depended on the world more than on God. What patterns, beliefs, or habits have promised peace but left you empty? What does it look like for you, today, to place your hope back into the hands of Jesus?

Scripture Reflection: *"Those who hope in the Lord will renew their strength. They will soar on wings like eagles; they will run and not grow weary, they will walk and not be faint"* (Isaiah 40:31).

Waiting on the Lord is not weakness; it is trust. When we release our need to strive, control, or perform, God renews what has been worn thin by effort and fear. His strength lifts us beyond exhaustion and into a steadiness that does not depend on circumstances. Hope in Him does not drain us; it restores us.

Scripture Promise:

"Be still and know that I am God" (Psalm 46:10).

"My peace I give you. I do not give as the world gives" (John 14:31).

"I sought the Lord and He answered me. He delivered me from all my fears" (Psalm 34:4).

Prayer:

Jesus, I release every counterfeit source of hope. I surrender every place in my life where I have relied on my own strength or the promises of people. Heal the parts of me that have been shaped by striving. Break every false truth I have partnered with. Fill me with Your peace. Anchor me in Your presence. Teach me to trust You above every other voice.

You are my hope.
You are my truth.
You are my rest.

Amen.

CHAPTER 18

WHEN THE FIRE FELL

The days that followed felt like living inside the book of Acts. The same God I had read about, the One who opened prison doors and made the blind see, was now moving through a laptop screen, through Wi-Fi, through surrendered hearts gathered across the world.

It didn't matter that we were separated by oceans and time zones; the Spirit made us one. In that sacred digital sanctuary, we became the living Body of Christ, breathing with one heartbeat. When one person wept, we all wept. When one person was delivered, freedom rippled through every square on the screen. We were one body, one family, one sound, Heaven's symphony rising through bandwidth and fiber optics.

The world outside waited, unaware that a quiet revolution was happening, not in cathedrals or stadiums, but in living rooms and bedrooms, where the remnant gathered in obedience. The healing that began in that unseen sanctuary would become a wildfire, transforming hearts, homes, marriages, and generations. And as the healing transformed us, the Kingdom expanded.

There was no denying it: Heaven had invaded our rooms.

One by one, the students began to encounter Him in ways that defied reason. Tears flowed freely. Faces softened. People who had carried decades of shame suddenly erupted in laughter, not forced laughter, but the kind that comes from the marrow, the kind that only joy unspeakable can bring.

It was as if every heart had been waiting for this exact moment, the moment they'd stop performing and simply receive.

I didn't have a curriculum for what was happening. I didn't have a script. I didn't have the right words. All I had was obedience.

And somehow, that was enough, because God didn't need my perfection. He needed my yes.

The atmosphere in those trainings became thick, alive, trembling with holiness. You could feel the fire of the Holy Spirit rolling through like waves, wrapping every person in the gentleness and power of a Father's embrace.

Deliverance began to happen in ways I could have never imagined, not through theatrics but through the authority of peace.

And then, like a domino, the miracles began.

A woman who had battled infertility for years conceived within months.

A marriage that had been on the brink of divorce was reconciled.

A man plagued by chronic pain for over a decade woke up pain-free.

These weren't stories of hype. These were testimonies of Heaven.

It was undeniable. The same Spirit that raised Jesus from the dead was right here, redeeming what had been stolen, right before our eyes.

Every session became holy ground. Every Zoom call became a tabernacle. Every participant became a witness to the living God.

There was no more striving, no more self-help, and no more "finding your truth." There was only one Truth. And He was setting His people free.

As I led, I often felt my knees buckle beneath me, not from fear, but from awe. The Presence would come so thick that I could barely breathe. My hands would tremble. My heart would pound. My cheeks would burn as if they were pressed against the flame of God Himself.

It wasn't chaos. It wasn't frenzy. It was order. It was holy. It was peace that passed understanding.

I realized then we had become a move of God.

Lighthouse wasn't a brand or a business. It was a living altar, a divine invitation for His glory to dwell.

And when the fire fell, I didn't just watch people transform. I watched *myself* transform.

All the pride, the self-striving, and the need to be seen burned away.

All the residue of performance and proving, gone.

In its place was purity, reverence, stillness, and power.

The girl who once stood behind a microphone every month, selling art for a million dollars, was now holding space for Heaven to touch Earth.

And as I stood in that holy silence, watching deliverance after deliverance unfold, I heard the Lord whisper again the same words that started it all: *Redeem the ground.*

Tears streamed down my face as I realized what He meant all along. He hadn't just redeemed the training. He had redeemed *me*.

The same hands that once chased profit now trembled with purpose. The same voice that once sold paintings now proclaimed freedom. The same woman who once performed to be loved was now loved beyond performance.

The fire had fallen, and nothing, not one single thing, would ever be the same.

Reflection: When the fire of God fell, it didn't fall on one person. It fell on a *people*.

Just like the upper room, it came to rest on those who waited, hungry, surrendered, and unified, not self-seeking, not competing, not performing, but becoming one heartbeat in the Spirit.

It wasn't the eloquence of words or the perfection of structure that moved Heaven that day.
It was the sound of unity. A remnant crying out in unison, *Here we are, Lord. Use us.*

In that moment, the power of the Body of Christ became more than a verse I'd memorized; it became a living, breathing revelation.

When the Body moves in harmony, healing flows. When one part rejoices, all rejoice. When one heart repents, the ripple delivers others. When one person forgives, generational chains break.

This is what the world doesn't understand about Kingdom power. It isn't about self-help, self-love, or self-healing; it's about *surrender*. The fire doesn't fall on self. It falls on sacrifice.

Every time the Body comes together in unity, whether in a living room, a Zoom call, or a sanctuary, the Spirit rushes in to inhabit His people. And the world outside, unaware of the miracle happening inside, can only stand in wonder at the fruit: marriages restored, children healed, nations changed, and hearts set ablaze.

When the Body is one, the Kingdom expands. And every time the fire falls, Heaven finds a home again.

Journal Prompt: Where am I still trying to do life, faith, or healing alone?

Declaration:

I am part of the living Body of Christ.

I am not an island; I am a member of His heart.

Where I go, His Kingdom goes.

Where I speak, His voice is heard.

When I forgive, chains break.

When I love, healing flows.

I will not hide my light under the container of fear or performance.

I will burn in unity with Heaven and with my brothers and sisters on earth.

We are one heartbeat, one flame, one family, one Spirit.

Scripture Reflection: *"How good and pleasant it is when God's people live together in unity... for there the Lord commands the blessing"* (Psalm 133:1, 3).

God's fire falls where His people are one. When the Body of Christ gathers in unity and surrender, Heaven responds with power, healing, and life. Unity is not just agreement; it is the place where God chooses to dwell.

Scripture Promises:

"When the day of Pentecost came, they were all together in one place… and they were all filled with the Holy Spirit" (Acts 2:1-4).

"For just as the body is one and has many members…so it is with Christ" (1 Corinthians 12:12).

"How good and pleasant it is when God's people live together in unity…for there the Lord commands the blessing" (Psalm 133:1, 3).

"May the God who gives endurance and encouragement give you the same attitude of mind toward each other…so that with one mind and one voice you may glorify the God and Father of our Lord Jesus Christ" (Romans 15:5-6).

"And the glory which You gave Me I have given them, that they may be one just as We are one" (John 17:22).

CHAPTER 19

THE COMMISSION: THE FIRE STILL FALLS

What began as a practical decision rooted in Phill's work and complicated visa realities slowly revealed itself to be something far more intentional, far more precise, and far more sacred than we could have understood at the time. Borders, paperwork, waiting seasons, and uncertainty became the very tools God used to move us where He wanted us, not according to our plans but according to His timing.

Canada was never the destination. It was the hiding place.

For two and a half years, God held us there, not as punishment or delay, but as protection, as though He was placing us under His own hand while He stripped away everything that was unnecessary, everything that was loud, everything that could not survive where He was about to send us next. What looked like a detour from the outside was actually a divine pause, a season of refining that no amount of momentum or ambition could have replaced.

It was there, in the quiet weight of waiting, that God grounded me deeply in His Word, removing my reliance on platforms, approval, and visible fruit, and teaching me how to hear Him when there was nothing external to affirm that I was on the right path. He was not preparing me to build yet. He was preparing me to carry what would be built.

Only after Canada did Texas come.

And when we finally crossed back into the United States and set foot on Texas soil, the difference was immediate and unmistakable. The air felt heavier, saturated with glory and purpose, as though the land itself carried memory. Light poured gold across everything it touched, and even the wind seemed to whisper promise, reminding us that this had always been part of the plan, even when we were hidden far from it.

This was not simply a move. It was a relocation of destiny.

Texas was not just a new place to live. It was holy ground, soil prepared for legacy, the land where Heaven would meet earth in visible ways, and where the Kingdom would expand through those willing to say yes without clarity, comfort, or guarantees. What God had refined in Canada would now be planted in Texas, not rushed, not shallow, but rooted deeply enough to withstand multiplication.

Canada refined us. Texas commissioned us.

And only then could I see how every closed door, every visa complication, every forced pause had been orchestrated by a God who never wastes a season. He hides before He reveals. He roots before He multiplies. And He never releases what He has not first secured in Him.

This was not an accident. It was the unfolding of a promise.

Even now, I can feel the tremble of what is coming. Heaven is preparing a place for encounter, a sanctuary where the body will rise as one. I can see the faces, radiant and undone, as the Spirit of the Living God moves among them. I can hear the sound of deliverance, the cries, the laughter, and the freedom song that only Heaven can compose.

It's not a matter of *if*, it's already alive in the unseen. The gathering has already been written in eternity. The altar is being prepared. The oil is ready. The fire is waiting for breath.

When the people assemble, it won't be a conference. It will be a convergence. Heaven will bend low. The body will unite in one heartbeat, one Spirit, and one sound. And the Kingdom will expand, unstoppable, uncontained, and unashamed.

This moment exists outside of time. It belongs to eternity.

The world calls its teachings "containers," as if the light of God could ever be contained. But the Kingdom of Heaven doesn't live in programs or protocols. It lives in fire: wild, pure, and untamed. The Holy Spirit doesn't need a structure to move. He needs a surrendered room.

What the enemy built as a cage, God turned into a sanctuary. What was meant to manipulate became a place of deliverance. I watched as the false light faded and the true light broke through, unstoppable and unashamed.

Because you can't contain freedom. You can only host it.

The world doesn't need more influencers; it needs *intercessors*.

It doesn't need more self-help; it needs *surrender*.

It doesn't need another trend; it needs *truth*.

Now more than ever, the call is clear for obedience over popularity. Holiness over comfort. Repentance over reputation.

We are living in an hour where the Church must rise, not just in belief, but in boldness. Not just in attendance but in authority.

We are not called to conform to the ways of this world, but to *transform* it through the power of the Kingdom. To bring Heaven to earth. To make disciples of nations. To preach the gospel, not of man's improvement, but of God's dominion.

This is not a call for the casual believer. It is a call for the consecrated, those willing to be purified in fire so they can carry glory. It is a call to the brokenhearted, to the brave, to the ones who have been refined by pain but still refuse to bow to the world's idols.

The Kingdom is recruiting. The Commander is calling. But before you can march onto the front lines, you must be healed.

You cannot cast out darkness while you are still making peace with your own. You cannot carry the sword of the Spirit with a fractured heart.

This is why Lighthouse Global Ekklesia exists. This is why "The Academy" was born.

It is the Kingdom's training ground, the sacred space where warriors are made whole, where hearts are restored before hands are sent. It is where sons and daughters remember who they are: anointed, appointed, and chosen for such a time as this.

You cannot walk in your calling until you've healed from your past. And you cannot fight for the Kingdom until you've let the King reign in every part of you.

When the true gathering happens, it won't look like religion. It won't sound like performance. It will feel like breath returning to dry bones. The body of Christ will rise, not as fragmented parts, but as one heartbeat. Each person will carry a spark until the whole room ignites into a holy wildfire.

The world outside will wait as Heaven moves within us. The sound of worship will thunder like waves. Healing will pour like oil. Deliverance will erupt like song. And every soul present will know that the Kingdom of Heaven has come.

This isn't imagination. It's revelation. It's not what's coming; it's what's already unfolding in the unseen. God is raising a remnant that cannot be bought, silenced, or contained. The Church is awakening. The Bride is rising. The fire still falls.

In the quiet, when the lights are low and worship has faded into silence, I know what I'll do. I'll stay behind, palms open, face lifted, heart trembling. The air will hum with His presence, thick with the fragrance of oil and tears. And I'll whisper what I've whispered a thousand times before: "Lord, what now?"

And He will speak, not in thunder, but in a whisper that fills every part of me. His voice will come through mine, steady and certain.

The Final Decree

My daughter. My son.
You have walked through the fire, and you have not been consumed.
You have wrestled with darkness, and now you carry light.
You have been broken open, not to be destroyed, but to be remade in Me.

The world told you to find yourself, but I came so that you would lose yourself in Me.
You are not your past. You are not your pain. You are not your mistakes.
You are My vessel of healing. You are My chosen instrument of revival.

The fire still falls, not to destroy, but to refine.
Go into the world and speak My truth with boldness.
Love the unlovable. Forgive the unforgivable.
Be mercy in motion. Be hope on display.

Do not hide the light I placed in you.
Do not contain what I designed you to release.
You are My hands. You are My heartbeat. You are My voice.

The Kingdom of Heaven is not coming someday; it is here now.
It lives in you. It breathes through you.
Go and set My people free.

I stayed there for a long time, kneeling on the floor, tears soaking the wood beneath me. The silence was holy, not empty, but alive. The presence of God lingered like fire in my chest. I knew the truth deep in my spirit.

The fire never stopped falling.

And as I stood to my feet, I knew this was only the beginning.

Reflection Questions: Where do you sense God calling you to build, plant, or begin again?

Journal Prompts: Write about a moment in your life where you knew God was calling you to more, even if you did not feel ready. Describe the tension, the fear, and the unseen courage that rose within you.

Declaration:

I am a carrier of God's fire.

I am refined but not destroyed.

I walk in obedience, not opinion.

I choose holiness over comfort and surrender over self-reliance.

The Spirit of God burns within me and goes before me.

The Kingdom of Heaven is alive in my life.

I am anointed, appointed, and commissioned for such a time as this.

I will not hide my light. I will not bow to the world.

I rise as a warrior of the King.

The fire still falls, and I am willing to be set ablaze for His glory.

Scripture Reflection: *"For our God is a consuming fire"* (Hebrews 12:29).

Fire purifies. Fire refines. Fire reveals. The God who met Moses in flame, who fell on Elijah's altar, and who filled the Upper Room with tongues of fire is the same God who prepares His people today. His fire is not a punishment. It is an invitation. It is the marking of those who dare to walk in obedience rather than comfort, consecration rather than compromise, and surrender rather than striving.

Texas was not simply a geographical shift. It was a spiritual commissioning ground. A place where the fire fell, not to destroy but to ignite purpose. God still directs His people through whispers, winds, and burning ground beneath their feet. His call remains unchanged.

Be holy. Be bold. Be surrendered. Carry My flame into the world.

Scripture Promise: *"And your light shall break forth like the dawn, and your healing shall quickly appear"* (Isaiah 58:8).

This is the promise for every surrendered heart.

When you obey, light comes.

When you yield, healing comes.

When you rise, the Kingdom rises with you.

And the fire that falls on you will set others free.

CONCLUSION
I STILL HATE GOODBYES

If you've made it to these final pages, then you've walked with me through shadows and into the light. You've witnessed what only the mercy of God can do with a surrendered life. I am not the person who began these chapters, and if this book has done what it was meant to do, neither are you.

And yet, even now, I'll tell you the truth.

I still hate goodbyes.

Not in the way I once did. Not with panic gripping my chest or fear convincing me that separation meant abandonment. Healing has done its work. Jesus has done His. But there is still a moment when my heart skips, just for a breath, when someone I love walks away.

When my husband leaves for a business trip.

When I used to watch my children walk into school before we began homeschooling.

When someone drops me off at the airport or I turn and watch them disappear through security.

There is a flicker. A memory. A sensation that reminds me of where I've been.

The difference now is this: I recognize it.

I no longer confuse that feeling for danger. I no longer let it narrate my story. I lean into the strength of Jesus and quietly name what it is: a healed place that still remembers. A nervous system that once learned love could leave. A heart that once had to brace itself for loss.

And instead of spiraling, I anchor.

I breathe Him in. I remind myself that love does not disappear when someone walks away. That connection does not dissolve with distance. That I am not being abandoned. I am simply being trusted to stand.

Healing did not erase my tenderness. It redeemed it.

Even as I write this, I feel it again.

I don't want to say goodbye to you.

Which is interesting, because I likely don't know your name, your face, or your story in detail. And yet, something rises in me, the same familiar pull to keep close those I've shared my heart with. To linger. To make space. To say, *Stay just a little longer.*

This used to come from fear.

Now it comes from love.

A love that has learned how sacred connection is. A love that understands that vulnerability is costly and therefore holy. A love that knows when hearts meet in truth, something eternal happens, even if the moment is brief.

Every word you've read was breathed out in partnership with the Holy Spirit. There were days I wrote through tears, through trembling, through awe. I didn't write this to tell a story. I wrote it as an act of obedience. To testify to the One who saved me. To expose the lies that kept generations bound. To remind you that freedom is not a concept.

It is a *Person*.

This book is not an ending; it is an invitation.

An invitation to step into truth.

To surrender.

To be refined.

To let the fire of God burn away everything that isn't you.

The same God who rescued me will rescue you. The same Spirit who hovered over the chaos of my life hovers over yours, ready to create something new, something holy, something alive.

If you feel the stirring, the trembling, the pull, it's because Heaven is calling your name. You were made for more than survival. You were made for dominion. You were made to bring Heaven to earth.

So no, this is not goodbye.

It's simply the moment where I trust you to continue walking. With Him.

I can't wait to meet you. Maybe it will be in a Lighthouse training room, under the glow of worship, or in a quiet moment when the Holy Spirit reminds you that you were never alone.

He's still writing your story.

And the Truth, His Truth, will always, always set you free.

THANK YOU FOR READING MY BOOK!

Just to say thanks, I would like to give you a special bonus!

7 LIES YOU MAY NOT KNOW YOU BELIEVE

Scan the QR code here.

I appreciate your interest in my book and value your feedback, as it helps me improve future versions. I would appreciate it if you could leave your invaluable review on Amazon.com with your feedback. Thank you!

www.ingramcontent.com/pod-product-compliance
Lightning Source LLC
LaVergne TN
LVHW041332080426
835512LV00006B/424